DEAR COCO:
THE COFFEE TRUCK THAT CHANGED MY LIFE

by
Ant Duckworth

Contents

For my girls Emma, Malia, Lani and Coco.
You give me wings.

Foreword

Dear Coco: The coffee truck that changed my life chronicles the rollercoaster journey from Sydney to London of Ant Duckworth, Australian family man, surfer, international marketing director and dreamer.

Set between 2015 to 2024, Ant immerses us in his raw, tenacious journey to give his family a more adventurous life. The story starts with Ant's deeply emotional struggle with an unexpected pregnancy, and a mistake that splits his close-knit family between hemispheres. With nowhere to live and facing relentless professional and financial hardship, Ant must swallow his pride and step up.

Starved of inspiration and creative opportunities – and fighting a dangerous body image battle – Ant decides to risk everything. He empties his family's life savings to bring forward a retirement dream and save his mind (and bank balance) from collapse.

The result is Dear Coco Coffee, a coffee truck business built as a love letter to Ant's youngest daughter. This coffee truck goes on to rescue Ant's emotional health, save his family from financial ruin, inspire a global coffee community and be named one of the *Top 5 Best Coffee Trucks in the World.*

Ant brings us behind the curtain for an all-access look inside the coffee truck business, viewed by many as the toughest category in coffee. He shares his secrets to success, how much money his coffee truck makes and the multi-million-dollar investor circling his business.

Dear Coco: The coffee truck that changed my life is a family man's story of iron will and unbreakable spirit. People from all walks of life will see themselves in Ant and his relentless determination to succeed – an ambition we all possess in one form or another.

Grab a brew and enjoy.

"Every child grows up thinking their dad is a hero or a villain until they're old enough to realize that he's just a man".

-Mark Maish

Chapter 1
Decision #1. Standing on the Beach

From an early age I had my feet in the sand and bare chest on a surfboard. I had an idyllic Australian beachside childhood of supportive parents, loving older brothers and an amazing education. I had friends, freedom and role models.

Every day after school Mum would drive a car full of kids to the beach and watch us surf until dark, turning the headlights on when it was time to come in. We'd often pretend we didn't see the lights if the waves were firing that day. Mum worked all day at the local college and I'm sure sitting in the car after dark was the last thing she felt like doing, but she did it every day with a loving smile on her face. Once darkness fell we'd drive home sitting on beach towels, shower in our wetsuits, eat dinner and do our homework. We did this on repeat every single day, and I adored it. I was the olive-skinned, slender built, athletic young man that lived in the ocean, so much so my dark brown hair had permanent blonde tips from years and years of sun and salt water.

I was constantly surrounded by happy families and lots of mates. We ran free and wild up and down Sydney's Northern Beaches while travelling to as many surfing contests as possible to keep the cabinet stacked with trophies.

I became one of the best young surfers in Australia on competition merit, and the captain of the Warringah Rats rugby team. I had my first kiss at the age of fifteen and was never teased by my friends about not smoking the marijuana joints being passed around our circle on the beach every weekend.

I couldn't have wished or hoped for a more privileged, albeit simple, upbringing. I had everything I needed, I longed for nothing and to this day I feel incredibly lucky I was given this life. I was every bit the average Aussie kid who had to endure next to no hardship thanks to the hard work, love and protection provided by my beautiful parents Maralyn and Paul, and the deep friendship with my two brothers Chris and Simon, who I've looked up to my entire life.

My dad played a particularly formative role, showing me what a hard-working, stoic, honourable man could be. He set an example I wanted to live up to, not only there and then in my early years, but by setting a roadmap for the man I wanted to become.

In 1995 I graduated high school and went to university to study Business Management, second only to Arts as the most generic, non-committal university degree available. Back then, Business or Arts degrees were for people that didn't know what they wanted to do after high school, people like me. While studying full-time I worked at the Newport Arms Hotel as only their second-ever male bartender, given their hiring focus was attractive females. The first was Tony, a specimen of a man seemingly carved out of granite that the ladies adored. I was also store attendant at the local Liquorland, stocking shelves and selling bottles of alcohol and cigarettes.

~~~~

Fast-forward to 2015, and I was standing on Freshwater Beach on Sydney's Northern Beaches, now a thirty-seven-year-old doting family man. It was a sparkling summer morning and our two daughters were running in and out of the ocean, laughing and splashing around like a beach party scene out of *Home and Away*. To my right was my beloved wife. Emma is my dream girl; she's my oxygen and I adore her like no other. To my left were my daughters Malia (seven) and Lani (six) in their sun-smart rash vests dragging around my Morey bodyboard by its leash. It was 28 degrees Celsius with a light offshore breeze and knee-high waves. The kids were alive with joy and Emma and I had never been happier. This setting was many people's idea of utopia. I was living our own version of paradise.

The four-bedroom house we co-owned with the bank was a mere five minutes away. It's the family home I grew up in that Emma and I bought off my parents to fund their retirement and realise our own Sydney property ambitions, which for many people is an impossible real estate feat. We had friends and family littered all over Sydney's Northern Beaches; Emma and I have a blissful, happy marriage and our family had no issues we couldn't overcome. I was living my corporate dream as Marketing Director of a blue-chip organisation. We owned surfboards, two adorable cats, a car, and a Harley-Davidson. I had zero health issues and a full head of hair. Life was beyond sweet and I was deeply grateful for what we'd built.

But amongst my deep-seated gratitude for this glorious life we'd created, somehow I still felt a niggle. I had an itch I needed to scratch. It's a strange, counter-intuitive feeling not being entirely content with the utterly beautiful life that Emma and I had created. But here was the issue: standing on the beach that day gazing out onto the horizon, I could picture the next twenty years of my life playing out vividly. It was a vision full of happiness, gratitude and it brought a wry smile to my face. *How did such a humble guy who graduated high school and university, but is the very definition of average, get so damn lucky?*

So why change anything? I had everything I wanted and more. Why, standing on Freshwater Beach that day, did I suddenly feel the burning urge to completely upturn our lives? Some folks have to go away on expensive holidays to experience the lifestyle we'd created for ourselves, so why did I have this underlying feeling of dissatisfaction? Amongst some completely rational thinking here's what I kept telling myself: I'm uneasy about being able to picture the next twenty years playing out so clearly. Although it's a beautiful life and I'm deeply thankful for it, I reckon we have more adventure in us than this.

Before having children I travelled the world extensively. I visited over thirty countries; I lived in a campervan with mates and shared houses with strangers around the world. I loved and lost, worked hard, played hard and everything in between. Landlocking myself for the foreseeable future didn't sit well in my heart, not at thirty seven years old anyway. So, in that moment, without reservation or consequence, I turned to Emma and uttered the soon-to-be fateful words *"How would you feel about moving the family to London?"*

Confused about where the question came from, Emma naturally asked why. I told her about my thirst for more adventure; about giving our girls a European upbringing;

about returning her to her Northern Hemisphere motherland after thirteen years living in Australia (Emma is half British, half French and now an Australian Citizen). And how, by being in the centre of the highly revered European dessert making scene, she could not only continue but scale her fledgling baking business. I painted a beautiful picture of spontaneous long weekends in Paris, being anywhere we wanted within a two-hour flight from Heathrow and the girls learning to speak French just like their grandmother. The sales pitch was coming out like butter and it sounded like sheer bliss. Before I could contemplate the size of the can of worms I'd just opened, the dream was SOLD to the blonde in the flowery bikini. Without hesitation Emma excitedly answered *"Yes!"* and hugged me like we'd just got engaged.

Shit. In my spontaneous, overly decisive, early mid-life crisis moment I hadn't thought about what to do if she actually said yes. But it appeared we were now relocating a (currently) financially secure family that was (currently) on its professional ascendancy to a foreign country without any regard for what might or might not happen. I was now on the hook for something very big and very scary. Little did I know, I had just set in motion a series of events that would challenge the family and our relationship with each other like never before. These events would leave scars that would never completely heal, and cause financial devastation I never knew possible. I couldn't possibly have known there was something lurking beneath the surface that day on Freshwater Beach, waiting to pounce on the beautiful adventure we'd just committed to. But for now, we were moving to London!

As we busied ourselves getting our Sydney affairs in order – re-homing our two beloved cats and preparing the family home for tenants – we received some bombshell news. Emma was pregnant with our third child, and the age gap to the baby's older sisters would be seven and eight years. It completely knocked the wind and momentum out of me. In front of Emma I acted delighted with the news, but behind closed doors I was a crumbling, insecure mess. This pregnancy news wasn't in the script and it took a lot of processing. Just as we'd laid the foundation for our next chapter overseas, we now had to pump the brakes and rethink everything.

I felt shame in feeling like our yet-to-be-born baby had somehow just done us (correction, me) a disservice. I found myself asking some hard questions: *Isn't our family already complete? Do I have any more love to give another child? Do I want to go back to being a single-income family after financially struggling for eight years? Do I even want another child?* My mind couldn't stop racing with insecure, upsetting thoughts. These thoughts might not be entirely uncommon for those who've faced similar situations, but for me these feelings were incredibly confronting. These were extremely challenging questions to be asking myself amongst the ultimate joy of falling pregnant. Many people don't ever get to experience this joy, and here I was lucky enough to be offered it for a third time. The guilt of even pausing for thought hit me hard and it wasn't a nice feeling. I felt like a ticking time bomb ready to explode.

The war being waged in my mind eventually erupted to the point where I couldn't take the torment any longer. I needed to talk to Emma, she always made me feel better. One night after Malia and Lani went to bed, I physically broke down. I admitted to Emma that I couldn't face going through the process of being a new dad again. I cried inconsolable tears telling her the pressure I felt financially dragging this family through the last eight years, only to be returning to that feeling for another untold number of years. I told her I was suffocating under this new, resurfaced pressure and that I couldn't breathe. That I couldn't be a third-time father.

Through my own admission I'd created an impossible situation for Emma. I knew she was excited for our third baby, but I shamefully dominated the moment with my own selfish agenda. I was unhinged with my own vulnerability and showed no regard for how Emma was feeling about the pregnancy. Taking advantage of her supremely giving nature, I convinced her to consider our options. The option we landed on was to visit a family planning clinic in Chatswood, Sydney. I say we, but I actually mean me, and I hated myself for it.

The feeling I carried walking into the clinic that day, knowing it was against Emma's wishes, will haunt me until the day I die. It still causes me insurmountable, unspoken pain all these years later. I've buried this shame so deep inside I didn't think it would ever appear out in the open. I've never spoken about it privately or publicly. After sitting in the clinic answering the doctor's pre-qualifying questions, we commenced the intrusive and heart-breaking procedure. As Emma lay there in tears I'd never felt so small. I wanted to protect this woman from anything that could make her upset, but in this moment I was the one causing all her pain. As the doctor commenced the procedure she stopped and informed us we weren't ready to abandon the pregnancy just yet. The pregnancy was too early in term and the foetus wasn't developed enough yet. This meant the procedure wouldn't be happening that day, and we'd have to re-book the appointment and return in a few days. We'd be living with this crushing guilt for longer than we expected.

We left the clinic and went to get something light to eat. It had been an unbelievably draining day. Sitting in the food court of the nearby shopping centre we couldn't even look at each other, and it was all my fault. I felt an intense amount of shame for putting Emma through such a devastating experience. I didn't sleep a wink that night, and I turned away from Emma in shame as I tried to silence the inner demons corroding my mind.

When I woke up the next day everything had changed. I sat Emma down on the sofa and poured my heart out to the point of not being able to talk any more. I told her there was no way I would ever put her in that position ever again. I felt a level of shame I'd never felt before, talking her into something she didn't want but was willing to do to care for her husband's emotional health. I asked Emma to please forgive me, which she did unconditionally, and I told her I wanted to keep our baby. An instant love for our unborn child was formed that morning and has never faltered since.

This conflicting time brought Emma and me closer, but also challenged our togetherness. Ultimately, we made the right decision for us. Welcoming our new baby into our family would make us complete. My selfish agenda and resulting decisions I forced upon Emma, and the deeply confronting process that followed, left scars that we healed together. But my own scars of shame and guilt will never truly heal.

~~~~

As we prepared to welcome Coco into the family, I made the emotionally difficult decision to cancel our impending move to London. Relocating a young family to the other side of the world with a pregnant wife and no support system felt irresponsible, so we deferred the move indefinitely. Emma was shattered, she had already emotionally left for London and we'd re-homed our beloved cats at great distress. Taking this life adventure away at the eleventh-hour broke me. I'd let the reality of being a father for the third time stifle my adventurous, decisive spirit. I despised myself for it on top of the always-on guilt I was feeling from our pregnancy journey to date. I was not in a good spot at this point in my life – I was not my father's son – and I'd never hated what I saw looking back in the mirror until now.

In May 2016, Coco was born. She was absolutely perfect and today we can't imagine life without her. I set about being the most incredible third-time dad humanly possible. I took parental leave from my corporate job and immersed myself in falling deeply in love with Coco. I wanted us to become inseparable best friends, and we formed an instant connection. I adored this child, I stroked her face when she slept and cried the harshest of tears knowing I nearly wasn't the dad she deserved. I almost let her go, I almost didn't fight for her. From her first day to my last, this little girl and her sisters will now be at the centre of every decision I make. I wanted to over-love Coco; I wanted to cancel out the demons that conquered me before she was born; I wanted to correct the mistakes I made.

Little did I know in five years' time Coco would inspire a decision that would once again alter the course of my life. A metaphorical love letter I'd write her would transform me into the person I was desperately trying to be. But the decision would also force me to face the demons that for now I was pushing deep down where I couldn't hear them tormenting me.

Chapter 2
Homeless. Separated. Broke.

As Coco grew, my unquenchable thirst for adventure returned and I felt confident enough to suggest to Emma that we reinitiate our move to London. The passion and excitement that we felt eighteen months earlier returned instantly. Suddenly everything we'd been through over the past year-and-a-half was now worth it. I felt vindicated; I felt like the family leader; I felt strong again. So here we go again – we're moving to London!

We proceeded to do what most Australians moving to Europe do; we told our friends and family we'd be gone for two years. Spoiler alert, very few Aussies move to Europe for two years. The distance is so great and effort so immense that many stay for much longer. Yet we kept saying "*Just two years*" to make the people we left behind feel better, and ourselves feel less intimidated about moving to the other side of the world with three kids and no idea what lay ahead.

As we set our London plans back in motion, whatever it was that was lurking beneath the surface on Freshwater Beach eighteen months earlier started to get restless again. Unbeknownst to either of us, soon our London dream would begin to unravel, and unravel in epic proportions. Our dream was about to turn into a nightmare.

Like many Australians, I needed a visa to live and work in England, so months before we were due to depart Sydney I lodged my online application for a UK Spousal Visa. Everything was stacked in my favour and I had all boxes ticked I needed to qualify. I'm married to a British citizen;

we have three dependants who have British citizenship; we had enough money to satisfy all the financial requirements and I'd be continuously employed during the relocation process. Surely the visa application was a mere formality? I was so confident of this, I submitted the application online without the support of an immigration lawyer. Never could I have imagined the repercussions of this choice. The thing that had been lurking beneath the surface since that day on the beach just came up for air.

Weeks went by and my visa didn't arrive. Weeks turned into months and still nothing. *"Let's not panic"* I told the family, *"We still have time"*. But that time was drying up fast, our London departure date was looming and I still didn't have my visa in hand. No matter how many times I reassured Emma and the girls that it'd be here in a matter of days, I sensed something was drastically wrong.

As with any international relocation, we packed up our life to leave on a set-in-stone date. That date was in three days' time and my visa still hadn't arrived, so it was time to make a difficult decision. We decided that Emma would depart as planned with Malia and Lani – we'd done too much to postpone things at that point and our shipping container of belongings was arriving into the UK. I'd stay in Australia with one-year-old Coco until my visa arrived. Surely it would only be a matter of days, and we'd meet the family in London the following week. Coco and I waved goodbye to Emma, Malia and Lani amongst a flood of tears and open question marks. We all drank the optimistic Kool-Aid I was slinging and believed it was the right decision at the time. *"We'll see you soon"*, I said, not entirely sure that was true.

Days turned to weeks, and weeks turned to months. Our family was broken in half, separated against our will. No mother should be without her one-year-old baby against her wishes, and my beloved family who I cherish and would protect with my life was now sleeping on floors on both sides of the world, running out of money and asking people for help.

I was raising Coco on my own in Sydney while working full-time from my parent's apartment to keep money coming in. Emma was catching buses around London with two young kids in tow begging landlords to accept us as tenants, but without any UK income, and a husband stuck in Australia with visa issues, landlords weren't exactly chomping at the bit. As a result, Emma couldn't secure anywhere to live.

My family was separated, officially homeless and neck-deep in a bureaucratic mess. This wasn't the dream I sold to Emma standing on that beach. On the other side of the world to my wife, I was piling so much guilt and blame onto my shoulders the weight of it was crippling. Desperate, I called the UK Visa and Immigration Office every single night begging for an update on my visa application. Every time I'd call and get put on hold only to be told the application is 'In Progress' and no update was available. I was lost in a bureaucratic system so big and complex no one could hear me scream, nor even care I was screaming. I cried most nights after Coco went to bed; I walked down to the beach at night alone and screamed at the pitch-black horizon; I punched my fists into the sand thinking of my girls on the other side of the world not having a home.

In desperation, I decided to engage an expensive London immigration lawyer to help. We agreed a scope of work that would see us financially broke, but I had no other choice. At least now I had legal representation, shame on me for not doing it from the start. Within hours of sending our lawyer my existing visa application for his review, he phoned at 2.00am Sydney time and uttered the words that will sit with my forever...

"Ant, you will NOT get your visa. You need to bring your family back to Australia!"

Panic set in and I found myself shaking uncontrollably. It was now official, I'd let everyone down. The damage was devastating. I'd singlehandedly ruined our beautiful life.

I choked back tears to ask, *"Why won't I get my visa?"* and was told I'd fallen victim to a misleading financial requirement of relocating to the UK. I was set to earn money in the UK, paid by an Australian employer in Australian dollars into an Australian bank account. Nowhere throughout the visa application process did it say this wasn't permitted. The only condition was I needed a certain level of financial means to immigrate, which I thought I more than satisfied with my Australian income. The Home Office didn't agree and determined that I didn't meet the financial requirements to enter the UK. Emma didn't have a job lined up in London given she was on parental leave with Coco, so in the eyes of the Home Office our earning capacity at that moment was zero. The minimum annual amount required to satisfy the financial requirement to enter the UK was £18,600. What frustrated me no end was that I was currently earning enough money in Australian dollars, yet it counted for nothing; I needed to be earning this money from a UK entity. This was a disaster.

According to this shiny big city immigration lawyer that I couldn't afford, it turned out thousands of other visa applicants had unknowingly fallen into the same predicament. This initiated a Supreme Court action against the UK Home Office for unlawful refusal of thousands of visas. The reason why no representative from the Home Office would speak to me about my doomed application suddenly made sense – they simply weren't allowed to. I fell into the 'Supreme Court action' pile of applications, so they ghosted me completely.

I will never forget the feeling of sheer helplessness as I cried lying next to Coco that night, stranded on the wrong side of the world with no idea what to do next.

But I needed a solution, fast. My problem-solving mind went into overdrive. What resources and/or relationships did I have at my disposal? There was no way I was turning my family around and bringing them back to Australia. Not only would the financial consequences be disastrous, but everything we'd worked towards for the past eighteen months would be for nothing. We had tenants in our Sydney home and we'd re-homed our pets. We had dreams on the line and I was in full-on protector mode. I made some calls to my office and lined up a meeting; I left Coco with her Grandma and Grandad, donned my sharpest business attire and packed some tissues, this day was going to get emotional. I caught the 190 bus from Manly Beach into Sydney city centre. My destination was 242 Pitt Street, the corporate headquarters of Australia and New Zealand (ANZ) Banking Corporation, the employer I was planning to leave once our move to London was complete. But in that moment I needed ANZ to help me get to London; they were my only shot.

I'd mapped it all out in my head. Although it's an Australian organisation, ANZ Bank had a small International Banking Division based in Canary Wharf, London. This division was a UK legal entity. In my mind if ANZ could internally transfer my employment from the Australian organisation to the UK entity and pay me in British pounds I could satisfy the financial requirements of the visa. I would emigrate to the UK on something called a Tier 2 Intra-company Transfer Visa and once in London I'd re-apply for my Spousal Visa – applying from within the destination country brings a much higher chance of success. I'd then transfer off the Tier 2 Visa onto my Spousal Visa and resign from ANZ Bank with my utmost thanks and gratitude for supporting my relocation. Simple, right? No.

Although simple in philosophy, transferring between legal entities within a major Australian bank is not easy. It required the Chief Executive of the UK organisation to authorise the creation of a fictitious head count for the sole purpose of bringing a stranger into the London business. My salary would be internally journaled from my old entity to the new one. The fictitious role would report to no one on the organisation chart; I'd have a desk in the Canary Wharf office with no name plate or staff card to the office canteen. I'd have no colleagues, no responsibilities and no friends. I'd be an office ghost that existed only on paper. Trust me when I tell you this is not easy or logical. Banks don't like anything not logical, but this was my only option.

I stood outside 242 Pitt Street staring up at this ivory tower of hope. What I was about to ask of my boss had never been done before. This was my problem to solve, not theirs, but I selfishly and unapologetically made it their problem too. I needed to pull on the heart strings of an organisation that doesn't have heart strings. I went to the 12th floor and met my boss, Tracey, in our pre-arranged meeting room. Tracey knew I was having visa issues, but didn't know to what extent, she thought I was simply waiting for my Spousal Visa to be issued. This was going to be an emotional conversation and it needed to be the conversation of my life.

Step by step, I walked Tracey through the sorry saga. I told her the heartache Emma was feeling being separated from her baby and husband; I explained that my family was homeless in London because I screwed up the visa process. It all came out, every square inch of it, and I cried three months' worth of tears in thirty minutes. People rarely cry in corporate high-rise buildings so this was an unusual sight, so much so I turned my chair to face away from the confused colleagues staring at me through the meeting room glass.

The next five minutes have sat in my heart ever since. All my prayers were answered, and I'm not even religious. Tracey was one of those leaders that moved heaven and earth for her people. She had relationships at all levels of the organisation and managed-up exceedingly well. Put simply, Tracey got shit done. Really important shit. She looked at this broken Marketing Director sitting in front of her, put her hand on my shoulder and told me she'd solve this problem with me. Knowing the organisation the way I did, I knew Tracey was accepting a monumental task choreographing this difficult internal move to the UK organisation. I can't remember ever feeling this level of relief or gratitude towards any one person in my life. I'd felt completely lost and alone, buried in a bureaucratic mess with the UK Home Office for months. Tracey was the first person to reach below the water level and extend her hand. When I asked her why she was prepared to help me, it was evident good karma is a real thing.

Five years earlier I had been brought into ANZ Bank as an external hire to lead an Event Marketing organisation. The team I was hired to lead needed deep restructuring. This involved years of performance management, HR cases, cultural rebuilding, infighting amongst team members and unfair dismissal cases. You name it, I faced it. I inherited a miserable remit and it took its toll on me. Each morning I'd arrive for work on my Harley-Davidson and after getting changed into my business attire I'd stare at myself in the changing room mirror, willing myself to go upstairs. Picture Rocky Balboa while training for the Clubber Lang fight and you're about halfway there. It was a hellish time to lead a team, but I persevered and protected Tracey from the fallout.

I guess Tracey felt indebted to me for showing such resilience, and my tenacity bought me my plane ticket to my girls. Not only did Tracey execute the entire internal process, she also agreed to have Deloitte manage the entire project at the expense of the organisation. Just as well too, as I'd just spent our entire life savings on that immigration lawyer I couldn't afford. Deep compassion and precedent-setting actions are rare in organisations like major banks. Tracey, supported by her senior leadership team, will forever hold a place in my heart.

A condition of the deal was I needed to fly to Byron Bay, about two hours north of Sydney, to deliver one final project before I left for London. With Coco still in my full-time care, and the length of time I needed to be up north we decided that Emma would fly back to Sydney, collect Coco and head straight back to London. I'd then fly to London from Byron Bay once the project finished. So we did just that – Emma left Malia and Lani with loved ones and flew thirty three hours from London to Sydney. Coco and I met her at the airport amongst a flood of tears – they hadn't seen each other in months and it was the most beautiful reunion I'd ever seen. All three of us stayed the night in the same bed in a local hotel before Emma got straight back on another thirty-three-hour flight to London with Coco strapped to her chest. What a woman she is.

Two weeks later I was on a plane to London to be reunited with my family. Relief coursed through me. Nothing could go wrong now.

Chapter 3
Welcome to London. Mind the Gap

Arriving in London I knew no one. I had no little black book and no professional Rolodex.

I've always said my home is where my girls are, so London was now my home. But all the other niceties that come with home were missing at that early stage: friends, connections, familiarity, routine. Starting with a blank sheet of paper and designing the life we wanted from scratch is an adventure and the appeal of moving countries, so I was not only *not* intimidated by these livelihood gaps, but energised by them.

Amongst all this newness I still had my day job to do. Every morning I boarded the empty, almost eerie District Line at Turnham Green at 5.00am and made my way to the ANZ Canary Wharf office. I needed to be sitting in a teleconference room with my game face on by 6.15am so I could get two to three hours' overlap with Sydney business hours, where my team and senior leadership was located. I'd enter the ANZ building while the cleaning crew still had mop buckets dotted around the lobby and the night security guard was on his fiftieth game of *Solitaire*. We'd wave hello as I stumbled through the main foyer clearing the sleep from my eyes. I wonder what position they thought I occupied to justify such early morning starts –Vice President of International Markets; Kitchen Porter; Technology Concierge? Whatever their presumptions I'd walk in each morning like I owned the place. It was the only time of day anyone even noticed I was there.

I spent the next few months as a ghost in the London office. I spoke to no one; they had no idea who I was or why I was there. It was a lonely existence but a necessary step in my long-term goal of staying in the UK. My lawyer continued the process of transitioning me onto my hard-fought, long-awaited Spousal Visa. But this visa remained elusive. The process resulted in me having to leave the UK to buy myself as much time as possible while avoiding spending more than 180 days on the Tier 2 Visa. If I did then I was liable to pay double tax on my Australian earnings, something I most certainly couldn't afford.

I needed to find a way to exit and re-enter the UK at virtually no cost given our current financial predicament. I found an opportunity to teach English for free on the outskirts of Madrid. It was the cheapest way for me to leave and re-enter the UK for tax management purposes. The role of Volunteer English Teacher (paid only in flights and accommodation) was an unbelievable experience. Adults of all ages, walks of life and countries of origin would invest heavily in these seven-day immersive retreats where they were only allowed to speak English amongst themselves and the volunteer teachers. It was thought seven days of speaking nothing but English would equate to months of self-directed English study back home. They were motivated to learn and I was deeply motivated to teach them. I respect anyone who invests in chasing a dream, so I was all-in to help them accomplish theirs.

Towards the end of the retreat I was voted the group's favourite teacher by a landslide, which felt like a real honour. According to the students it was a combination of things that contributed to this accolade. They said I had an unwavering level of commitment and attention to them as people and their overall learning journey. Teaching English is mentally fatiguing for the teachers as well as the students, so it's only natural by the end of the week that both started to fade in energy and enthusiasm. The students told me I was the only teacher that remained 100% committed and energised from day one to day seven, and they loved me for it. They also said my accent was the easiest to understand. Normally Aussies get accused of lazily eating our words when speaking, so this feedback put me on cloud nine. During these retreats I made some brilliant friends. It felt energising to start building connections in the Northern Hemisphere away from Sydney.

Concurrent to my work in the ANZ London office and this trip to Madrid, my UK Spousal Visa process was reaching its crescendo. My London-based lawyer, who I'd now spent many hours with in-person in his Thames-side offices (which explained his exorbitant fees), was ready to submit my application. I was unbelievably nervous about the success of this new application for a few reasons. Given my original UK visa application was rejected, there were some question marks on whether the Home Office would raise a red flag against the alternative settlement route I was now seeking. The Senior Partner of the law firm reviewed my case prior to it being submitted to the Home Office and saw 'no logical reason' why it should be declined. This didn't entirely fill me with confidence – illogical visa decisions seemed as prevalent as logical ones – but it was as close to a vote of confidence as I was going to get.

I was seriously up against it from a timings perspective with my 180-day deadline looming. There was no way I could absorb this extra tax liability given our current circumstances, so we needed to get my Spousal Visa in hand before the 180-day milestone was reached, now only a few days away.

Given the time pressure, I needed to pay an exorbitant processing fee to receive a same-day visa decision, which involved a face-to-face appointment at a UK Visa & Immigration Centre. The only visa centre at which my lawyer could secure an appointment within the time frame was in Glasgow, Scotland. I searched behind the sofa cushions for enough money for an early morning EasyJet flight from London to Glasgow, tucked the 2,000 page visa application under my arm and off I went with five days left on the clock.

That day I successfully secured my hard-fought Spousal Visa to remain in the UK. We'd done it! I'd emerged victorious from a system so brutally complex and soulless I could hardly contain my emotions. I immediately recalled standing on Manly Beach months earlier punching my fists into the sand in frustration. Nights and nights of tears cried as I lay next to Coco separated from my family, feeling completely helpless. All this was now a thing of the past, vanishing as a distant memory only to reappear as I recount the tale for this book. I was now a permanent resident of the UK, dependant only on Emma continuing to have me as her husband, which was just about the only thing I was confident wouldn't change any time soon, touch wood.

I called Emma and the girls to tell them what we'd just achieved. None of them could comprehend the journey we'd just endured, and once I hung up the phone I cried as hard as I can ever remember crying. In some downtrodden, industrial estate on the outskirts of

Glasgow, an Australian father of three felt like the richest man alive.

~~~~

With my Spousal Visa secured, it was time to say goodbye and thank you to my leadership team at ANZ Bank. They will forever hold a special place in my heart.

From that moment on I was out in the professional wilderness. I was faced with rebuilding my career without any local contacts or relationships. I was starting from scratch, but for me that's part and parcel of starting a new life in a foreign country. I set about laying dozens of irons in the fire, interviewing around London as the new-in-town external candidate who knew no one. I was repeatedly taken to final round interviews only to be used as the external benchmark for internal promotions. This went on for weeks and the frustration and panic started to build as I faced a very worrying reality. I couldn't secure a job; the family was within a few weeks of being completely out of money and I had no UK credit card to fall back on. This was serious – just as we got over the top of one hurdle (my Spousal Visa) I now had another monumental hurdle to contend with. But I'm a strong, resilient, capable person who backs himself in any situation, so I pushed on hour after hour, day after day looking for the job that would save our family from financial collapse.

My daily job search routine involved scouring the jobs board on LinkedIn along with other job-seeking websites. The LinkedIn algorithm seemed to throw up job vacancies well suited to my skill set, along with many that weren't. Given the volume of mismatched job opportunities being suggested to me I applied my own filter of only looking at job postings newer than seven-days old. I figured anything older than that would already have 2,000+ applications.

One morning I was sitting in my favourite Chiswick café job-hunting while Coco doodled on a napkin. As my thumb scrolled through hundreds of postings that didn't suit my own filtering technique, my phone screen seemed like it was stopped in place by a higher power. A role titled 'Senior Manager, Global Experiential Marketing' within one of the world's most powerful brands appeared right in the middle of my phone, and it felt like fate. The company advertising the job was American Express. I had no idea what experiential marketing was until I read the job description, but it sounded like a great fit for my experience in event marketing. In parallel, I had also started an application for a similar role within a global wealth management organisation, Morgan Stanley, and British multinational bank, Barclays.

After submitting all three applications I was fortunate to progress through round after round of interviews for all three roles. Each round brought a new interview with more demanding interviewers occupying increasingly senior roles within each organisation. The interviews were appropriately tough, and I hoped my desperation wasn't too obvious as I received call-back after call-back. I remember asking myself what new intel could they possibly discover at interview #7 that they didn't already know at interview #6? But that's the process when applying for vacancies like this – decision by committee is how these multinational organisations roll.

Eventually and remarkably, I made it to offer stage for two roles, which took a level of performance I was deeply proud of. But there was an underlying problem, as both roles were lower in seniority to what I left back in Australia, and there was a significant pay gap. But I had no choice; I had to take the best opportunity for growth and worry about money later. A pay cheque and potential for advancement were my most pressing priorities, in that order.

Not long afterwards I started my new role as Senior Manager within one of the world's most recognised and powerful brands, American Express. During my onboarding process I was told my first pay cheque would arrive in 5 weeks' time, so it was two-minute noodles most nights for dinner for a while. Things got extremely tight financially during that period of time, and often Emma and I would go to bed hungry to ensure the kids' tummies were full.

So there I was, I had a job in hand and my first pay cheque was on the horizon – my only way now was through. Mine was a new role within the organisation that didn't exist before I was appointed to it, so I needed to educate the American Express EMEA organisation on the value of experiential marketing and forge new relationships at all levels of the organisation. In short, I needed to be so damn good that I positioned myself for a promotion to a director-level role that didn't even exist. I needed to command that role be created, and when it was I needed to ensure it was awarded to me. I had to not only perform at the level I was hired, but I also needed to plant seeds that would reap rewards in the not-too-distant future.

For sixteen months I worked my corporate hands to the bone, including twenty-two trips into Continental Europe to deliver a level of marketing expertise the region had not seen before. I won hearts and minds; I built relationships; I attracted visibility at the senior leadership table; I became well known and respected across Europe. I was branded the 'Mayor of London' by my US-based Vice President – she was astonished by the impact I was having in all corners of the EMEA region. I was a man on a mission, I simply had to make Director.

No matter how hard I worked or tenaciously I pushed, the financial hardship started to bite, and bite hard. Unable to climb out of the financial hole created by our relocation and subsequent immigration issues, the family simply couldn't survive on my current American Express salary, and I needed to stem the financial bleeding fast. Emma was studying food photography while looking after three displaced kids full-time, one being two-year-old Coco, so it was an issue I needed to own for the family.

On a dark, rainy London evening on my way home from the office, dressed in my full business attire, I faced a soul-destroying reality. I had no choice, I walked into the local pub and asked if I could tend bar three nights a week. I've never shied away from hard work or positioned myself above any job, but this was work I did at university twenty years earlier. Only this time I'm forty years old working for minimum wage while losing almost half to tax as a second job. But I simply had to make ends meet. The Assistant Bar Manager I spoke to didn't know what hit her. As with everything I do, in applying for the job I recounted the story of my professional and personal life like my future depended on it. Fifteen minutes later she folded my CV in half, smiled from ear to ear and welcomed me to the bar staff team. I don't think she could believe her luck; an ex-Bartender/ex-Bar Manager/ex-Restaurant Manager/ex-Group Operations Manager was now her grossly overqualified new Bartender at minimum wage. The job I'd just accepted would earn the family £4.30 per hour after tax. It wasn't anywhere near enough to take the pressure off, but it helped buy groceries.

From day one I performed my bartending duties in utter secrecy. I avoided eye contact if any neighbours or new friends walked into the bar. They always appeared shocked to see me working behind it. But at that moment I was my father's son again; if I'm doing a job I want to perform it to the best of my ability, no matter how tired or overqualified I am.

I tackled this bar job like every other job I've had in my life. I gave it my absolute all; I left no stone unturned and performed like my life depended on it. While the other bartenders were leaning on the bar hungover and tired, I was running cases of beer up and down the narrow stairs from the cellar, banging my head on the low beams consistently found in old British pubs. I served customers; emptied bins; cleaned toilets; polished glasses; mopped vomit off floors and re-set tables. I wanted my daughters to be immensely proud of me, so I immersed myself in being the best forty-year-old bartender I could be. I wanted to be able to stand hand-on-heart and recount my own journey of tenacity and iron-clad work-ethic when my girls become old enough to take a similar job. I wanted to become undeniable, both in my corporate and bar staff lives.

As a result of my efforts, I was named Pub Employee of the Month for months on end. I was twice the age of any other staff member, the only father of children and was operating on the least amount of sleep out of anyone. But my obsessive work ethic wouldn't allow me to operate any other way. I became a kind of father-figure to the group of young bar staff, and they looked up to me for what I was doing for my family. There I was working side by side with colleagues half my age and earning half the hourly rate these kids were making. This will- power earned me enormous respect and street cred in their young eyes, and their admiration made me feel validated for twenty hard-fought, gruelling hours per week.

~~~~~

December rolled around, the second in our new house, and I was invited to our neighbour's Christmas party at their glorious house, next door to the humble maisonette we occupied. We lived in the quintessential worst house on the best street, surrounded by highly successful people who came from money old and new. It was safe to say I felt socially and financially out of my depth from when I left my house each morning to when I returned home at night.

The evening of the neighbour's Christmas party I entered the already-underway soiree, where everyone seemed to stop and stare as I came into view from the front door. The host put her arm around me like I was the sympathy invitation from next door, which was not the intention of the invitation but it's how I felt at the time. The well-to-do guests looked at me like I was Mick Dundee amongst the New York City glitterati. *"Isn't that the guy from the pub up the road?"* I could hear being whispered by the Chiswick elite. As I was handed off by the host to make new acquaintances, it was clear I had nothing in common with the other guests. I may as well have been from another planet.

I wasn't aware at the time, but well-off British people *love* talking about education, specifically private school education. They're obsessed with it. Almost every conversation I muscled into at that Christmas party circled around which private school we intended to send Malia to next year. When I mentioned we'd be utilising the public school system a past-his-prime grey haired gentleman patronisingly said *"Ah good man, putting those tax dollars to good use ey!"*. I felt like shit the entire party; I felt small; I felt totally out of place. Rarely in my life have I walked away from an uncomfortable situation, but I escaped out the back door and jumped the fence without anyone noticing I was gone.

Living in Chiswick I wrestled with deep insecurities. Feeling like the poorest guy in one of London's most affluent suburbs, I didn't feel like I belonged. We chose Chiswick because it had an immaculate reputation for making young people feel safe. Many parts of London deter young people, in particular young girls, from doing simple things like wandering the High Street with their friends, or using public transport after dark. Like many cities, parts of London just don't feel safe after dark which can stifle the enjoyment of teenagers starting to crave their independence. For these reasons we chose and ultimately adored living in Chiswick, but it didn't do my ego or self-confidence any favours living amongst people I didn't consider my peers.

Working two jobs, seven days a week meant I was burning the physical and emotional candles at both ends, and I never saw my family. This wasn't the dream I sold to Emma on Freshwater Beach, it wasn't even close. Surely there was some light on the horizon? There had to be.

~~~~

In August 2019 my relentless efforts were rewarded in my corporate job at American Express. I had achieved my goal. My US-based Vice President, on recommendation from the Chief Operating Officer in London, created a new position and I was the guy they wanted for the job. I was promoted to Director, International Experiential Marketing leading teams in Europe, Asia-Pacific and reporting to New York. I was now back to the same seniority level I was when I left ANZ Bank in Sydney, and I was beside myself with emotion. Yep, you guessed it – I cried tears of joy not unlike those cried by Will Smith's character when he was appointed Associate at the end of *The Pursuit of Happyness*. A promotion at this level normally took 4-6 years to achieve, if at all. I did it in sixteen months as an external hire while bartending in secret three nights a week. To say I was proud of myself was an understatement.

The family was now breaking even financially with my new corporate salary, so I immediately quit my bartending job with great thanks for taking on an old-timer. The feeling of freedom I now had not having to work Friday, Saturday and Sunday nights until 2.00am was immense, and I felt like we could now settle into building the London life I had promised the family before we left Sydney. But just as I got my feet under my new desk at American Express a major problem was brewing on the horizon. Something called COVID-19.

Chapter 4
'Ant x Joanna: Catch up'

In March 2020 the COVID-19 pandemic decimated my entire marketing channel, overnight and globally. I led an international team of experiential marketers that specialised in producing premium, in-person experiences for American Express's most important multinational clients. So it stood to reason mine was one of the first industries to collapse, citing 'an abundance of caution' (the term used to notify the external market when cancelling every global experience on the books). Whatever suitable, content-driven experiences remained were pivoted to virtual – where creative minds like mine go to die. Once the disappointing and financially disastrous process of cancelling millions of dollars' worth of in-person experiences had been completed, everyone within my profession braced for impact.

Industry colleagues and friends started getting laid off left, right and centre which felt inevitable – the events industry had ground to a halt almost overnight. There was no more work; event budgets were re-assigned to inject customer value in other areas and there was no predictable end in sight. Many event industry colleagues were freelancers so they were the first to be let go. Those on short or medium term contracts didn't last long either, and many full-timers had to quickly pivot their skills to prove their value.

As with many other large organisations, American Express gave public assurances of no COVID-related layoffs in 2020. This was an incredible, vital commitment for people like me and it made me feel somewhat insulated for a time, out of harm's way of what was happening outside. I was so deeply grateful that during the worst global storm to hit our shores in decades, I had a place where I could huddle and be safe, for now. *"But what happens when 1ˢᵗ January 2021 arrives?"* was the question that haunted me every single night, and I lived in fear for the next nine months. At every internal Town Hall meeting from March to December, this question was inevitably asked to the Senior Executive Team. All they could do was reaffirm the priority of protecting our colleagues during the eye of the storm, and when the New Year arrived the organisation would need to turn its attention to adjusting to the new norm, and re-build for growth. It all made complete sense and this was way more support than many people around the world were lucky enough to receive, so amongst the haunting feelings of uncertainty I also felt incredibly privileged.

But no matter how much privilege and gratitude I felt I wasn't immune to feeling vulnerable and exposed. I'd just got back to the top of my professional mountain after a wild few years, and I risked being knocked off my perch once again. But this time it was completely out of my control and I was merely a passenger along for the ride. To make things worse, my entire external industry was in utter ruins - if I got laid off from American Express there was nowhere to go, no one was hiring. The prospect of financial uncertainty was imminent yet again, and we had no family savings left after my immigration issues cost us everything. It wasn't lost on me that this situation was felt by many families around the world, but for me my world was my four girls and they were all counting on me to pull us through this uncertain time intact. The pressure felt immense.

~~~~~

1st January 2021 arrived like an unwelcome house guest. My senses were on full alert amongst an always-on feeling of nausea and anxiety. Every time I refreshed my work email inbox I dreaded receiving a short notice meeting invitation titled 'Catch up' with no agenda outlined. One of these meeting invitations almost certainly meant you're getting laid off, so people wanted one about as much as a hole in the head. I tossed and turned in bed every night hypothesising what I'd do if I got laid off. I'd put all my career eggs into one basket for the past thirteen years – I was in the business of in-person experiential marketing. Yes I had transferrable skills but trying to reinvent myself after being laid off in the middle of a global pandemic didn't sound too appealing.

And then the dreaded moment happened. There it was: 'Ant x Joanna: Catch up'. No agenda. *"Shit, that's it. I'm done"* I told myself. Where's the archive box to pack up my personal effects? This meeting invitation spelled disaster. I'm most certainly a dead man walking. I was physically shaking as I took the call only sixty minutes after receiving the invitation. Restructuring and displacements happen so fast in the corporate world.

Joanna, the Senior Vice President conducting the meeting, was pure class, the consummate professional. She did what schoolteachers do when calling parents during school hours regarding their child – she instantly reassured me things were OK. My role was not affected. She immediately put me at ease which I deeply appreciated given my heart and mind were racing so fast I barely even registered the rest of the conversation. What I did manage to digest was Joanna had spared me, but my direct leader and two peers were displaced amongst the

41

restructures needed to navigate the pandemic. These colleagues were close friends of mine, and their displacements almost certainly meant they would leave the organisation once the formal consultation process had concluded. The only thing that saved me from the same fate was I was the only Director on the global leadership team that led teams outside the US, so I was deemed not expendable as my role couldn't be consolidated with another. Lightning struck so close to me it singed my eyebrows, but ultimately missed me. I could keep fighting another day.

In the months following, multiple internal restructures kept the redundancy fear continuously flowing. Quite rightly, the organisation had to future-proof itself. Though technically secure, I was suffering under the weight of constant stress, uncertainty and with no outlets to focus my creative energy. I was in full-on survival mode.

~~~~~

To free my mind after lonely, stressful days sitting at my computer I started taking long, late night walks. Each night Emma and I would do homework with the girls, cook dinner and get Coco ready for bed. Once the routine was done I'd excuse myself from the house and vanish for hours on end. I'd walk 10-15 kilometres along the River Thames every night, wrestling with my inner thoughts and crippling levels of insecurity. I'd listen to music as I walked, trying to release the pressure. It felt deeply unhealthy to be living with a mind so full of anxiety, so these walks became my way of disconnecting from everything and everyone. I'd return home at 10.00pm or 11.00pm to Emma who was either in bed, or just about to turn in. This became my routine for months and it provided a welcome distraction, but what I didn't realise was the physical and mental damage I was unknowingly walking towards.

Prior to starting these walks my body weight hovered around 80kg. At 6ft 2 that weight was entirely appropriate for a man with a slender build. I naturally don't have much muscle mass, and at the time I carried a little extra weight around my midriff, not unheard of for someone in their forties who didn't exercise. I didn't love my shape, but it was the body I had after years of refusing to prioritise physical fitness.

As the hundreds and hundreds of kilometres of night walking passed through my shoes, I could see my body starting to change. I was getting leaner, and the excess weight started disappearing from around my waist. Weight loss wasn't the reason I started walking such long distances, but it became a by-product alongside the mental and emotional balance it was providing. I walked and walked and walked to quieten the demons in my mind.

Weeks passed and an opportunity came to take Malia to a London park so she could enjoy a picnic with her friend – they hadn't seen each other for a long time due to lockdown restrictions. I did what most dads do for their teenage daughters when meeting friends, I set myself up on a separate picnic blanket a hundred yards away. As I opened up my book, the mother of Malia's friend spotted me and stopped by for a passing hello. It was lovely to see her after so many weeks. We kept our distance when we would normally hug hello, but it was a sign of the times we were in.

As we exchanged pleasantries I could feel her looking at me in a slightly awkward, concerned way. It was clear she wanted to say something, but didn't quite know how. As the conversation progressed she mustered up the courage to say what had clearly been weighing on her mind. *"Ant, you are looking very thin"*. She said it with what felt like a heavy heart. This comment caught me completely off guard, and it was clear to my friend I wasn't expecting the remark. We said our goodbyes and she went on her way.

As she left I felt all sorts of emotions. I felt bruised, sad, angry and confused. Sitting on that blanket was a man who was no longer aware of himself. My appearance had prompted a personal comment from someone who felt compelled to say something. People normally tell others how great they look, not how unhealthy they appear to have become.

When I was sure no one was looking, I lifted up my t-shirt, wanting to inspect the typical fat roll that protrudes from most people's stomach when sitting cross-legged on a blanket. That fat roll was completely non-existent. All that remained were some tiny rolls of skin reserved for the leanest of humans, elite athletes or – dare I say – people suffering with eating disorders. I jutted out my elbow and looked at my bicep – it was down to the bone. Whatever minimal muscle mass I'd had previously eroded away. I wrapped my fingers around my wrist. My usual body weight made it impossible to connect the tips of my fingers, and now the fingers not only touched but overlapped. I pulled out my phone and took a selfie of my resting face. I looked gaunt and sunken. All of a sudden it became clear to me my friend was right.

Later, once our evening routine at the house was done, I set out for my usual walk. Only this time I wanted to walk further, much further. I was not only *not* concerned about the body realisation I'd been given hours earlier, but I now felt obsessed to lose more weight. Why? I don't know. So I walked. I ate smaller and smaller portions at every meal. I would stand naked in front of the mirror and pinch non-existent rolls of fat, pulling the skin down to convince myself I had more weight to lose. My mind told me the more weight I lost the better I looked. For weeks this battle played out in my mind as I weighed myself twice a day to see how much weight I was losing. Each night I would set off and try to walk further than the previous night. I was becoming obsessed to be the skinniest version of myself, which was completely counter-intuitive given I'd been the skinny kid who dreamed about being more muscular growing up.

As the weeks rolled on, standing in front of the mirror I could see every abdominal muscle, my entire rib cage and chest bones. The excess fat that once sat around my waist was now replaced with sharp hip bones. My clothes no longer fit and my appetite was a shadow of its former self. Yet my mind kept telling me to keep walking, keep losing weight, so I did. My 80kg body withered away to a dangerous 67kg. I looked under-nourished and unwell.

I ignored the loving outreaches of a concerned Emma asking if I was eating enough to fuel these long walks - I knew she was concerned about me but I was lost in an alternate reality. When she asked me how much I weighed I would inflate the number so she wouldn't worry. It was clear I was losing a significant and dangerous battle of the mind. Perhaps lying to Emma about my weight was hiding an   addiction   or   disease   of   some   sort.

I don't recall when it happened, but it's as if I woke from a comatose state and my mind clicked back into reality. Suddenly I was aware of my surroundings and I could see the damage I had done to my body. It was devastating. *"Enough Ant. Enough now"* I could hear my mind saying.

With hindsight and a clear head, I think about what was potentially going on back then, and I keep going back to how I had no control over my life at that point in time. I was at the mercy of everything and everyone, and I was carrying a lot of anxiety. Walking immense distances was perhaps my way of controlling whatever controllables I had left. Looking back now, I would support a diagnosis that I was self-harming in a state of derealisation.

I see photos of myself taken during that period and I feel deeply upset, but also intimidated by my distorted perception of reality. Standing in front of that mirror at 67kg I could literally see an obese man who still had weight to lose. Demons took over my mind so dramatically that the concern of a friend not only *didn't* bring me back to reality, but it spurred me on to self-destruct even further. I now have immense empathy for anyone who suffers with body image, derealisation or eating disorders. I'm an iron-willed, rational, mentally strong man who has never faltered, yet this thing took hold of me like I was a feather in the wind.

~~~~~

Throughout this period I still couldn't dispel the angst I was feeling amongst the continuous uncertainty surrounding my professional career. *"This can't be my life"* I'd tell myself. I felt like I was frozen. I hated not being the master of my own destiny, it made me feel powerless and exposed. I needed to take proactive steps towards owning some of the narrative around my professional life during such a disruptive, crazy time.

On those long walks in the dark I devised ways of creating a metaphorical safety net for the family. My mind raced with options. I had the creative brain space, the will power and street smarts to be doing more. But what could I do when the world was essentially closed and we were only allowed out of the house for limited reasons? Then the epiphany happened – a lightning bolt that would actually strike me and not just singe my eyebrows. I had an idea that could very well change my life and my family's lives forever. The guy who hates plans now had a plan, and a pandemic-proof plan at that. I felt an immediate and powerful new purpose. Little did I know what I was about to unlock.

Chapter 5
Decision #2. Standing in the Kitchen

In December 2020, a month before I was due to discover my corporate fate, I made a proactive decision. It was a freezing London evening and the kids had just left the dinner table – Emma and I made sure we ate together as a family every night to feel connected amongst the pandemic-related angst everyone was feeling. We had the kitchen to ourselves so I stood up from the table, I always perform better standing up. I told Emma I needed to talk to her about something important, and whenever I do this a look of concern mixed with fear washes across her face. I'm rarely serious to the point of needing a formal chat, so whenever it happens Emma suspects it's something big.

I closed the door separating the kitchen to the rest of the house to provide some uninterrupted privacy away from the kids. I wanted to focus Emma's attention on the conversation and not the pile of dirty dishes that I'd get to at some point. I was now centre stage, exposed and already too far along to call it quits. The spotlight was shining squarely on me.

I started to peel back the onion, layer by layer. I took the story all the way back to the start of the pandemic and told Emma everything I'd been feeling for the past however many months. I told her how vulnerable, scared and emotional I'd been. I told her I'd been struggling under the weight of visible and invisible pressures. I told her my confidence had been rocked, that old fears of not being able to financially provide for the family had re-opened, and that I needed to take some control of my life back. She either knew or suspected most of this already given the

48

closeness of our relationship, but it was good to capture everything in one spot to create context for what was coming.

Once I'd articulated how I'd been feeling, I turned my attention to the idea I'd had to try and future-proof the family amongst so much lingering uncertainty. I needed to create an image so clear and compelling that it would leave no room for hesitation or doubt. I was in full-on storytelling mode, my old self was back and I loved the energy that was flowing through my body. The conversation crescendoed with me asking Emma for the most trust I've ever asked in our eighteen-year history. Trust, I might add, should have been in short supply after the less-than perfect execution of my London vision only two-and-a-half years earlier.

I asked Emma for her blessing to invest our hard-fought life savings in a pipe dream. Savings we'd clawed back tooth-and-nail since climbing off the financial canvas. This pipe dream had lived so quietly in my head that Emma knew nothing about it. It came with significant risk and uncertainty in a time we already had those things in abundance. The timing felt reckless, but somehow that made it more powerful.

I revealed to Emma my dream-fuelled idea: build a coffee truck business to exist alongside my corporate career. But not just any coffee truck, the world's best coffee truck. Little did Emma know I'd already been saving this dream for when I was sixty five years old, retired and living on a beach somewhere. In the dead of night I would dream of being an old, weathered surfer serving other old, weathered surfers their morning coffee from a vintage coffee truck. This dream was set twenty years in the future but given the current circumstances I needed to pull the dream forward.

But why coffee? I spent the early part of my career managing restaurants, wine bars and cafés in Sydney, Melbourne and internationally. I led these businesses on behalf of private owners and large hospitality groups. I have hospitality in my blood and I'm damn good at it. I know food and beverages and I'm a master at customer experience. I've built and managed market-leading, holistic businesses from the front of house through to the kitchen and back office, I know what makes a successful hospitality business and I was particularly fixated on the coffee side of the industry.

And why a coffee truck? The romance of coffee trucks is undeniable. Who doesn't love seeing a coffee truck perched on the horizon like an oasis in the desert. No one will ever begrudge stumbling across a coffee truck as they go for a wander, and if you can take their breath away with an elevated experience they weren't expecting, then you've got something truly special. To clinch the deal, coffee trucks are outdoor businesses so essentially we'd be pandemic-proof.

Emma's blessing came instantly. She immediately bought into the vision I'd created – what a woman she is. She could see the energy and passion oozing out of my pores, the creative spirit that dominates me in normal times had flooded back. She could see the old Ant reappearing in front of her very eyes and she loved it.

~~~~

I had no idea what to do next, I hadn't done this before. I didn't have a formal business plan, SWOT analysis or even a napkin doodle. I'd done no due diligence, the business existed purely in my head, but I could visualise every tiny detail with total clarity. My mind raced all the way back to university where on day one of my Bachelor of Business Degree the lecturer insisted the FIRST step in building a successful business is creating a business plan. Eek, I don't have one nor do I see the value in it. *Writing a formal business plan will only slow me down,* I audaciously told myself. How many business documents are written with good intentions only never to see the light of day? Surely what's more valuable is I could see this business in totality in my head. I could see the Italian vehicle I'd convert, the plywood shelving display, the ceramic sugar pots, the glass display domes, the coffee menu, the espresso machine and the grinder. I could visualise everything down to the smallest detail. While doing my long evening walks I'd even found the perfect location for the business to trade.

To convince myself I was at least aware of how to build a business in principle, my lack of formal business plan became my 'business un-plan'. I didn't need investment from a bank or investor to build this business, so all this documentation felt like a redundant body of work to me. I hope my university lecturers aren't reading this, but this was my rationale and I stuck to it.

My first step was to find a UK company that could fabricate my Italian vehicle of choice, the Piaggio Ape 400 Classic, into the coffee truck of my dreams. I called a friend in the coffee industry and he tipped me off to a company in the North of England that specialised in converting vehicles into retail businesses. I called, left messages and sent emails, but sadly no responses came back – perhaps their business was buckling under the pressure of the pandemic. I didn't push and I moved on. I Google-searched a coffee truck company in Hull, England, that looked like they could help. I cold-called the office and had an amazing conversation with the owner of the business. He was so generous with his time and schooled me on the functional world of designing and building coffee trucks. He had an encyclopaedic level of knowledge of a well-designed coffee truck, so school was in session and I soaked it all up.

As we agreed to undertake my project together, I told him I might be different to other coffee truck owners he might work with. I needed to brace him for a different level of project without scaring him away. I laid out the vision, which to someone not connected to my broader story must have sounded overly confident, almost cocky. I told him I wanted to create a premium, elevated coffee experience on the street befitting the best London coffee bars. I told him this would be a challenging project that might deviate his company away from what they build day in, day out for other clients. I asked him to come on the journey with me to build one of the world's best coffee trucks. We shook digital hands and the first chunk of our £40,000 investment left our family bank account overnight, nearly every penny we had. This was an incredibly intimidating moment for me to put it mildly. I had just pushed all the family's chips into the centre of the Blackjack table and raised the dealer.

When I say I needed the truck builders to deviate from their usual turnkey process, I mean I demanded everyone involved in the project to think laterally. We needed to ensure our design, infrastructure and customer experience reflected the best London coffee bars, but on wheels. Decisions requiring lateral thinking came thick and fast. Typically coffee trucks in the UK use LPG fuelled coffee machines that deliver questionable quality to the customer. To illustrate the issue, very few self-respecting baristas want to work with LPG fuelled equipment, as it suggests a lower-quality coffee-making environment. The best cafés in the world use La Marzocco espresso machines, the Ferrari of coffee machines, built with love in Florence, Italy. So that's what I wanted, and there would be no debate.

But La Marzocco don't build gas-powered coffee machines, so I needed a stable form of electricity to power the entire business. This meant installing a generator, but not just any generator would do. I had the truck builders scour the UK for the most powerful, quiet, efficient generator that we could conceal within the belly of the truck so it wasn't visible to the customer. I wanted the generator soundproofed so the customer and barista didn't compete with the noise. I also wanted the lowest fume emission possible. This was new territory for the build team and there were moments I needed to have a few 'motivational chats' with the team to reinforce that it could and would be done.

My determination to install a La Marzocco coffee machine created an untold number of headaches, which brought an additional investment requirement of £4,500 to purchase and install the best Hyundai generator money could buy. If I was going to build a world-class coffee truck I could only install world-class equipment. If I was to attract the industry's best baristas I needed to provide the best tools. So the additional time and investment were well justified.

A design feature I insisted on was a pull-out, counter-levered floating bar. I wanted the customer bar to emerge from under the main counter and not touch the ground. This bar would be a major design feature of the truck so I was insistent it could be done. Much like the generator issue before it, a few motivational chats were required to re-engineer the under-counter framework and pipes to create space for the sliding wooden bar top. I also insisted on marine-grade plywood for the internal shelving and bar top. Unfortunately, however, the shipping container carrying most of the plywood being imported into the UK at the time got stuck in a canal…seriously, what are the odds! This brought the inevitable conversation of needing to move away from using plywood. My now infamous motivational chats meant the build team once again scoured the UK for enough plywood to complete our project.

I was so insistent on the design of the interior and exterior of the truck being perfect, I paid for the services of a Digital Designer to create a life-like 3D render of the truck. I wanted the build team to have a perfectly precise representation of what was in my head so no liberties could be taken.

I met with my London-based barista friends and mocked up our barista area to pressure test the workflow. I needed to ensure our future team could perform to the best of their ability in the environment I was creating. With some small tweaks we landed on the perfect environment for an incoming team, except for one functional problem. When the coffee machine sits next to the grinder, the steam wand shouldn't be on the same side as the grinder - the moisture created by the steam can affect the ground coffee. Luckily for me I had a mate who in his previous life in Sydney repaired La Marzocco machines as his profession. Once I purchased our new Linea Mini for the truck I shipped it to him where he spent many hours disassembling the machine and swapping over the steam wand and hot water spout so we could steam away from the grinder. This stroke of innovation captured the attention of eagle-eyed coffee enthusiasts who wondered why our Linea Mini looked different.

The build progressed as expected, and I walked the fine line of being an unreasonable client and one who inspired innovation within a traditionally turnkey process. My natural decisiveness and courage under fire went into a kind of chaotic overdrive. I was almost foolish in the pace and manner in which I was working. Challenges and setbacks came at every turn and I was overly decisive to the point of being reckless. Nothing would slow me down or get in my way.

In my haste I made and large and potentially damaging oversight. One thing I should have done even before I spoke to Emma in the kitchen was apply for council approval to trade. Street trading is a category where rules and regulations vary according to which London borough you're trading in. Some boroughs have a pre-determined number of 'designated pitches – these are fixed trading locations typically occupied by florists, fresh produce vendors and kiosks. The only way to secure one of these pitches is when the existing occupant vacates the pitch, which almost never happens due to their scarcity. When I enquired about the waitlist process for designated pitches in the surrounding areas around Chiswick I was met with a smirk from the Council Licensing Officer. She went on to say she had seen people on the waitlist for over ten years and never get to the top. Naturally this filled my heart with dread. I'd already invested £40,000 in our street coffee business, so I started to scramble. I enquired about what other kinds of licences might be suitable, and only one remained viable.

I decided to pursue something called a 'Temporary Street Trading Licence'. This process allows an applicant to find a location they thought suitable and apply to the local council for permission to trade at that location. The council would only accept applications for pitches that suited certain criteria, such as minimum 1.8 metre footpath width, traffic flow considerations, and the existing commercial landscape of the area. Once the council received approval from the owners of the land, local transport authorities and various council departments, the application would be made available to the local community to support or object based on whatever grounds they deemed relevant.

Concurrently, given I wanted to trade at our location more than twenty-eight days in a calendar year, I also needed to apply for Local Planning Permission, which brought with it the same community consultation process (and application fees) as the Temporary Street Trading Licence. Basically I needed two separate permissions that would ultimately grant the same approval, but generated twice the application fees to the local authority.

What I didn't realise at the time was that even if just one person in the community objected to either of the two applications, the matter would be referred to a local hearing. Unless the objection mounted by the community member had no merit whatsoever, odds were the council would lean in favour of the community and reject the licence application. All this information was new to me and the more information I discovered, the more nervous I became.

I surveyed dozens of potential locations for the truck in the lead up to submitting a Street Trading application, and all of them were unsuitable for a variety of reasons. Some didn't have enough foot traffic to make them financially viable; some didn't have wide enough footpaths to satisfy the licence requirements; some were too windy to make coffee; some were too far from home to drive our tiny vehicle to and from each day.

The one pitch location I found that ticked every box was opposite 85 Strand on the Green, Chiswick. In the months leading up to my decision to build a coffee truck business, I walked along this section of the River Thames on my long evening walks, so I knew this area well. I'd stop to take a rest on the river wall and stare at the six square metre patch of street, imagining what a coffee truck might look like in this beautiful riverside location.

Strand on the Green is a protected conservation area in West London. It's hallowed turf and stunningly beautiful. The glorious riverside homes look like they're straight out of a novel. Many local residents have old money, white-collar success and exemplary taste. Existing alongside them is a younger demographic of the community that works hard, lives well and values the beautiful things this area of London provides their growing families. Occupying the address of 85 Strand on the Green, directly opposite the pitch location, is the grand Steam Packet Pub, one of four riverside pubs dotted along this stretch of the river.

The pitch location had it all. The footpath was over three metres in width; the car traffic utilising the street was low to moderate; and there's a parking bay that runs the entire length of the street, perfect to park a coffee truck and not be an obstruction. There are no residential homes opposite or near the pitch, so whatever noise we'd make wouldn't impact any residents. And most importantly, the combination of local residents plus people who visited the area to walk along the river made it a well-pedestrianised section of the river.

In the absence of any kind of formal business plan I figured I needed some data to validate all the hunches I was acting on. On half a dozen occasions over a two-week period I sat on the river wall and physically counted people walking past. I'd count thousands of people and hypothesise how many I needed to stop to buy a coffee and a bake. To make the business financially viable I figured I needed to sell one hundred to one hundred and fifty cups of coffee a day, plus bakes and retail items. If we could get 5% of passers-by to purchase a coffee we'd be financially viable. This was purely back of the envelope maths, but it's all I had to bring some level of robustness to the investment process.

So that was it. Opposite 85 Strand on the Green, Chiswick, became the pitch location of choice for my so far nameless coffee truck business. I filled out applications for my Temporary Street Trading License and Local Planning Permission, submitted the applications according to the criteria set by the council and crossed my fingers and toes. Opportunities for community objection were posted at the pitch location by way of notices strapped to a lamp post, as well as inside the local newspaper. The community had four weeks to object. I called the Licensing Officer every two days asking if anyone had lodged an objection so I could emotionally prepare myself. I rang so often the Licensing Officer started to recognise my number and answered the phone with *"Hello, Ant"*.

Once the four-week consultation period had concluded I eagerly (and nervously) awaited my decision letter, which would arrive via email the following business day. As luck would have it, the email arrived while I was in the local supermarket shopping for ingredients for dinner that night. This supermarket struggled with mobile phone coverage, so when I saw the notification I dropped my already full basket of groceries and ran outside where phone reception would allow me to open the attachment. It was a twenty five page legal document and all my eye searched for was the simple word 'Approved'. I scanned every page trying to find that one magical word, but I was moving way too fast to find it.

My heart was pounding as hard as I could ever remember. *What happens if the application is declined?* I asked myself. I'd invested £40,000 before I'd secured a trading location for the business, and before I even knew what the requirements were. I'd be a laughingstock to those who didn't know our story of financial hardship, and a devastating failure to my family who would have to endure the daily impact of my oversight. My heartbeat got faster and faster. Then I saw it. Buried on page 24 in unassumingly small print amongst other legal jargon I couldn't understand were the words 'Permission is hereby granted'.

Months beforehand I'd stood in some downtrodden, industrial estate on the outskirts of Glasgow and cried as hard as I can ever remember crying. That day it was the car park of Sainsbury's Chiswick that would witness an Aussie bloke crying like he'd just won the Super Bowl. At that moment I realised the immense risk I'd taken in not doing proper due diligence before investing our life savings in a dream. I told myself to never put the family in that position ever again, no matter how confident or decisive I felt.

It was official, we were in business. Our official trading address was Opposite 85 Strand on the Green, Chiswick, London W4 3NN. It's not quite the beachside scene that featured in my retirement dreams, but it was absolutely the next best thing.

~~~~

As the truck build was nearing completion, the time to print the business name on the side of the vehicle was approaching. Late one night, I lay in bed scrolling through potential business names in my mind; this was a big decision and one that would set the tone for our business. I must have written two A4 pages full of potential names. Some were OK, some were passable, most were terrible. I wasn't connecting with any of them from an emotional or marketing perspective. Then out of nowhere the lightning bolt struck me right in the heart. I decided to name the business 'Dear Coco', a love letter to our now five-year-old daughter. It was emotional, personal and it connected the family to the business. The elevator pitch was crisp, humanised and went something like this:

"Dear Coco is built as a love letter to our five-year-old daughter, Coco. Given the age gap she can't work on the business like her two older sisters can so we named it after Coco to make her feel loved and included too".

In this moment the context behind the Dear Coco business name was pure love and marketing gold. But as the months and years passed, and my emotional walls began to crumble, this business name would take a heartbreaking turn to account for my sins of the past. Only time would bring this realisation to the surface, but I wasn't emotionally intelligent enough for that level of clarity back then. Naming the business Dear Coco would become the single most important decision I made for the business. The name and subsequent digital storytelling would go on to unlock an industry-agnostic brand presence and inspire a generation of coffee and non-coffee entrepreneurs around the world.

My mission was audacious: to elevate the entire coffee truck category in London. To deliver a premium, elevated specialty coffee experience on the street. Put simply, I wanted to take people's breath away; I wanted to capture their imagination; I wanted to be the best. I now had the physical truck, industry partnerships, trading location and business name to make this dream a reality. But working as hard as I was I'd taken my eye off a crucial ingredient to delivering under pressure over an extended period of time – my personal wellness.

Little did I know building a business while also leading an international team of marketers for a global brand would be so incredibly intense. I didn't get a single day off in five months. Physical and mental cracks were starting to appear, and my invisible demons that were lying dormant started getting restless.

Chapter 6
Dear Coco Coffee

On 6 May 2021, Dear Coco Coffee launched along the River Thames in London. It was a rainy Thursday, terrible conditions to launch a new outdoor business, and I was physically shaking with fear. As I drove the truck to the river that morning my mission was clear – treat this business like it's our family's saviour. It must work; I must be successful; I've put too much on the line to fail. I cannot fail.

Even though I'd managed multiple restaurants, cafés and bars on behalf of owners throughout the early stages of my career, this street coffee business was new territory for me. Simultaneously I needed to be a business owner, world-class specialty coffee barista, rapport builder and aspirational public figure. If I can't do any one of these things then we're dead. Hospitality businesses operate with impossibly thin margins, all it takes is a few quiet months and it's all over. These thin margins mean I must be good, really good, right from the start.

This pressure meant I lived with an always-on feeling of exposure. I had a crippling level of vulnerability to deliver on the promises and investments I'd made, and never had I felt so much pressure on my shoulders. In my corporate life I managed millions of dollars' worth of investments, but when its £40,000 of your own money representing almost everything you had, it's a very different feeling.

Day one along the river was nerve-wracking to say the least, but at least I wasn't alone. The Head of Wholesale from the coffee roastery that would supply coffee beans to

Dear Coco worked alongside me to ease the pressure. He performed the role of Lead Barista to free me up to introduce myself to our new community, take customer orders, serve the bakes and manage the queue. Although the rain deterred a good portion of our estimated foot traffic, those who stopped by experienced what I hoped they'd experience as I articulated my vision all those months ago. I wanted to stop people in their tracks and I wanted to take their breath away. The customer reactions to the physical aesthetic of the truck and the coffee being crafted within it exceeded whatever expectations they might have had. The entire day had a beautiful, positive energy about it and I adored standing on the street meeting our new Chiswick coffee community.

Our first trading day delivered £340 in sales which wasn't a disaster, but things needed to get a lot busier to be financially viable. I hoped that would come with time, this was only our first day and it was a rainy one at that. Our second trading day arrived and once again I had the support from the coffee roastery, however as the morning coffee rush calmed down my temporary Lead Barista gave me a high five and left me to it - he had other business he needed to tend to. Now standing alone on the street I felt way out of my depth, I was still a barista in training! Making coffee to a queue of onlookers is an intimidating experience even for the most seasoned baristas, let alone the new guy who has the weight of the world on his shoulders. But I turned on my trademark positivity, took deep breaths and reminded myself its one coffee at a time. *Don't rush Ant, it's more important to make 'em perfect than make 'em fast!* This was what I'd tell myself on repeat for the rest of the day, and it worked a treat.

Amongst the pressure of being a one-person operation that had to make coffee, manage payments, serve bakes, restock shelves and keep everything clean, I made sure to create space for a tactic I employed right from the start, one of the most impactful things I would ever do for the business. Very few things make someone feel more welcome than greeting them by name, especially when in their mind there's no way you could possibly remember them. I wanted to be the guy who remembered everyone's name and not just their coffee order, which counterintuitively is easier to remember than a customer's first name. From the minute we opened on 6 May, I introduced myself to every customer by name and asked for theirs in return. The minute they left the truck, and no matter how long the coffee queue was, I'd open the Notes app on my iPhone, write down their name and some descriptive words to remember them by.

Brad – nice Aussie bloke, big muscles.
Simon – white hair, restaurant owner.
Tom – glasses, owns small petrol station and land.
Jamie & Julia – lovely rich couple from SOTG (Stand on the Green).
Joe – nice salesman, Northerner.
Annabel & Tom – awesome smiley couple.
Shane – happy Irish guy, buys bags of beans.

To reciprocate the feeling and help our new customers remember my name, I printed *'Ant (Coco's Dad)'* on the left-hand side of my apron so it was visible below the level of my shirt, jumper or jacket. I wanted my name tattooed on their minds as the new coffee guy along Strand on the Green, and give them a hand if they couldn't remember my name after I'd just remembered theirs. This simple, personalised tactic of welcoming customers back to the truck with their name was so powerful. On only their second visit and amongst the sea of new people I was meeting, our new community was amazed how *'Ant (Coco's Dad)'* remembered everyone's name. The local WhatsApp groups blew up with instant love for their gorgeous new coffee truck and its Founder who was trying his hardest to fit in.

My two-hat work routine was exciting and energising but extremely demanding. I worked seven days a week consisting of full-time corporate hours compressed over Monday to Thursday, followed by Friday to Sunday as the Founder and Lead Barista of Dear Coco. It was non-stop and relentless. The determination and stamina required was like nothing I'd experienced before, but I HAD to make it work. Every day I'd drink my proverbial can of cement, harden up and get on with it. My financial goal was simple – replenish the £40,000 I'd invested (risked) from our life savings. I employed no one, I couldn't afford a payroll. I did everything myself and I didn't pay myself a cent - it was all about rebuilding the family's bank balance. Even though I wasn't working for free, not receiving tangible, immediate recognition for my energy by way of a weekly or monthly pay cheque was bloody hard at times.

The always-on stress of corporate life amongst continuous pandemic-related uncertainty and internal restructuring was intense. On top of this I was building a new business under significant emotional and financial stress while needing to appear completely poised. It was the kind of hustle I'm equipped to deliver, but the intensity was something I'd not faced before.

Every day I laced up my shoes and bound into my day with exuberance and purpose. No matter how tired or fatigued I felt I told myself this was my choice. It was never 'I *have* to do this'; it was always 'I *get* do this'. I'm the one who decided to create this life, so who am I to tell people how tired I am? In my career I've been fortunate to work with some of the world's best in their respective fields, but I've also been exposed to many at the other end of the professional spectrum. The people I relate to least are those who always respond with *"tired"* or *"busy"* when asked how they are. We've all been around these people, no matter what their actual state or condition they say they're tired like it's a badge of honour. Of course, it's entirely appropriate to feel tired and fatigued; I'm referring to people who use this response on repeat, every day. In my opinion this is a terrible personal brand to wear, so I've always made a conscious choice to go the other way. I choose to wear resilience as my badge of honour and reserve those moments of genuine exhaustion to show vulnerability. That was a time of my life where I needed to practice what I preached every single day.

~~~~~

As I dove into the world of social media for business, I needed to learn from a standing start. I was the guy who had created less than a dozen Instagram posts in his life, with about the same number on Facebook. I was not an active user of social media, I didn't know how to 'work the algorithm' or appeal to the masses. I followed people I cared about to stay up to date with what they were doing, and I followed a handful of professional surfers who posted great surfing clips. It was safe to say I was a novice in this space. I'm an analogue man in a digital world, but with a deep appreciation for the power of social media when used for good.

My marketing experience definitely helped me understand how I might share Dear Coco with the world, and I decided on a unique and very intentional brand voice. This business would be an open, vulnerable, authentic storybook that connected people to the origins of our business and brought people inside my mind. Our digital presence needed to be about more than just a coffee truck – I mean who really gives a shit about a plain old coffee truck? It had to be about something deeper, something that people could emotionally connect with no matter where in the world they were. There's only so many people who can and will experience Dear Coco in-person, so the digital version needed to be as compelling and real as if they were speaking to me at the truck.

Some brands forget that customers are human beings well before they're customers, so I took the human-to-human approach in how I would talk about our business. I marketed Dear Coco how I would talk to friends around the dinner table late at night, deep into a bottle of red wine. I am what my friends and family have labelled me for decades, a storyteller – so I tell stories from the coffee truck. I talk about family; about being a regular guy trying his best; about the daily grind of doing things most people aren't motivated to do. I call myself a regular guy doing irregular things. Our in-person customers and digital audience get a front row seat into my life and no topic is off limits. I call a spade a spade; I take a position; I have an opinion. But all the while I'm tactful, polite, sensitive and raw.

My approach to social media was an instant hit. Dear Coco quickly became the new, intriguing kid on the London and global coffee scene, and the industry took notice. The global coffee community immediately wrapped its arms around us, and social media influencers came running to 'discover' us. I'd never been tagged in a post before creating this business account, so this took some getting used to and involved me asking my Instagram-savvy wife what the heck was happening, and if all this is a good thing.

People came from all over London for our coffee and conversation. The Chiswick resident WhatsApp groups lit up. A wealthy single mother turned up at the truck in a chauffeur-driven car after flying in from Milan. She had a Dear Coco coffee, took some selfies and flew straight back home. A world-famous coffee artist flew in from Taiwan to interview me. La Marzocco, the Ferrari of coffee machine companies, interviewed me for their global coffee series. Podcast invitations came streaming in, local websites came running, parent groups wanted to talk to me about being a hard-working father who stopped at nothing to provide for his family. We were featured in Pretty City London, the bible for all things perfect in London, and the world's most prestigious brands wanted to work with us. It was mental! My dream was turning into reality, fast.

The business was trading just three days a week, which is all I was capable of since I worked the other four days in my corporate job. I strategically took annual leave whenever brands wanted Dear Coco for their media or customer activations. I needed to balance prioritising our street coffee customers while also building a strong brand, earning more money and diversifying our revenue streams through private bookings. It was a delicate juggle, but one I feel like I got right. Everything was working brilliantly, and much to my and Emma's surprise I paid off our £40,000 initial investment within five months of opening just three days a week – I originally projected it would take fifteen months. This milestone unlocked the next big opportunity to continue taking Dear Coco to the next level – we could now hire our first ever team member.

Anna was a barista in my favourite local café in Chiswick, so I knew her as a customer which is to say I didn't know her well. Aside from already knowing Anna was a world-class barista I also knew she was an actor, and a damn good one at that. One day my phone rang and it was the organiser of a prestigious urban design event being held in Kings Cross in a couple of weeks. He explained that this major event would attract the world's design industry media; the most prestigious brands would be exhibiting and tens of thousands of visitors would be attending. He needed a coffee truck to occupy a prime position outside the main exhibition marquee. It was still early in the phone call when I'd heard everything I needed to hear – this event aligned perfectly with the ambitions of Dear Coco, so I told him I'd be delighted to support. We shook digital hands and away I went to commence planning the logistics behind the scenes.

Given the volume of people expected over the three-day event I would need a professional barista working side by side with me for the duration. I was still new to the coffee industry at the time, so I needed some support connecting me to some suitable baristas. Worst-case scenario was I could always log the job with a barista temp agency like *Baristas on Tap*, but I wanted to see who I could find through my own network first.

I sent a text message to the manager of my favourite café in Chiswick and asked if she knew anyone who might want three days' work in Kings Cross. She immediately mentioned Anna, who had just resigned from the café to focus her time on her acting career. I sheepishly dropped Anna a text message with the three-day offer, having never spoken with her outside our existing barista-customer relationship, and she was delighted to help.

For the duration of the event Anna and I had a blast. We made some unbelievable coffee together. But most importantly I really enjoyed spending time with her, and it was a bonus that she was a phenomenal barista who represented Dear Coco so brilliantly. On the eve of the final event day I told Emma I believed I'd found the perfect inaugural barista for Dear Coco. Anna would be an ideal member of our team, but I also wanted to respect that she had just left her barista position to concentrate on her acting career.

I rarely get nervous, but that day I felt nerves as the final hour of the event approached. I knew I wanted to offer Anna a casual role at Dear Coco, but I felt shy asking. Acknowledging she wouldn't want anything too time-consuming I gingerly offered her the opportunity to work with us one day a week, and I would work the other two days. Anna appeared honoured to be asked, the proposal suited her acting commitments so we agreed and hugged it out as the inaugural Dear Coco team of two. What a way it was to finish a brilliant three days in Kings Cross.

The next week Anna turned up at the truck for her first shift on the street. As luck would have it the wind was howling and the rain was tumbling from the sky – the worst possible conditions to perform the role of street coffee barista. I was frustrated this was going to be Anna's first experience along the river, but it also ensured a baptism of fire that would only get better from there. Since Anna had already worked at the truck during the Kings Cross event the onboarding process was short and sweet. She felt very comfortable as Lead Barista, and after wishing her a happy shift I set off along Strand on the Green on foot, headed for home. About fifty metres down the road, in the pouring rain I turned and looked back towards the truck. A queue had already started to form and it was immediately clear that Anna was managing the scene expertly. Customers were smiling under their umbrellas as Anna set about building instant rapport.

In that moment, seeing a world-class barista standing at my coffee truck nurturing the business like it was her own made me incredibly emotional. Up until that moment I was the only barista our customers knew. I had endured the utter loneliness and exhaustion that came with building a one-person business. I'd made investment and design decisions that I hoped one day would appeal to highly credentialled baristas as a place to work. Day after day I stood completely alone on the street, working tirelessly to mould this business into reality. And there Anna stood, leading the next chapter of our business. I will remember this moment of joy forever.

Not long after Anna joined I decided to scale the business to trade five days a week. I could certainly use the additional profit this would generate and it was clear our customers wanted more Dear Coco, more often. To deal with the increased schedule I hired a team of guest baristas. These team members already worked in other cafés, but took whatever shifts became available that Anna didn't want. This was an ideal way to grow the team without committing to a certain number of shifts per month. This original team remains a treasured, valued part of Dear Coco to this day.

~~~~

Dear Coco was well and truly flying. I sat proudly opposite my family at the dinner table each night recounting the stories of the day and the global waves we were making digitally. The kids innocently hung off my every word like we were in a dinner scene from *Leave it to Beaver*. With our expansion to five days a week came the need for me to overlap Dear Coco with my corporate job every Wednesday and Thursday. When we only opened on Fridays, Saturdays and Sundays I could keep the two careers separate, but now I needed to work even harder to make this new rhythm possible but also sustainable.

This new routine would involve me waking up at 5.00am on 'workdays' to take the truck to the river. I'd set the truck up with the barista, exchange high fives and jump on the Underground to either my home office in Chiswick or my American Express office in Belgravia, Central London. Once my workday concluded around 7.00pm or 8.00pm I'd return to the river to collect the truck. Once at home I had ninety minutes of clean-down and re-stock procedure before I could finish my day. This new set of demands took my already exhausting work schedule to new heights, and I became fearful I'd committed to a routine that I wasn't capable of delivering, short or long term.

As a result of this new rhythm a silent danger now loomed in the shadows, watching over me as I worked, something I couldn't escape no matter how quickly our cash register rang or Instagram followership grew. The faster I ran the quicker it caught me. I was now firmly in its sights.

Chapter 7
Behind the Curtain

Have you ever been held underwater against your will? Gasping for desperate breath while someone or something literally or metaphorically holds you down. Seeing daylight above while feeling like you won't make it up in time, only to reach the surface in the nick of time. And the moment your head emerges above the water you have to perform like nothing happened while being completely drained of breath. Surfers know this feeling well; new parents know it too.

Functioning at a high level while completely exhausted and disorientated from sleep deprivation or insomnia must be one of life's toughest silent battles. With the pace and pressure I was working I started to wake up repeatedly throughout the night, every night. I had so much running through my mind at all hours of the night that I tossed and turned before going to sleep, and I never reached a state of deep, uninterrupted sleep. My mind jumped between my corporate responsibilities, my small business, family matters and how I wasn't spending enough time with my family and friends. I had the weight of the world on my shoulders and I went weeks without a deep, refreshing sleep. The sleep deprivation began to corrode me from within.

There was no call for sympathy, no tiny violins, no motivational tapes. I reminded myself daily that I'm the guy who didn't HAVE to do this, I GOT to do this. But even with all the gratitude and perspective I felt it still didn't change the fact that I was the guy who had to keep going. I was on the hook for gigantic promises that I simply had to deliver on. I'd let my family down a few times over the past few years so I was hell bent on not letting them down again.

No matter someone's background or walk of life, everyone can relate to the feeling of being physically exhausted and under pressure - that's not a unique thing. However very few people will ever truly understand how hard it is being a street coffee barista. Crafting specialty coffee, which represents the finest 6% of the world's coffee beans, is an art form. Serving this artisan coffee outside in a cold country like the UK takes physical and mental toughness. Imagine a hairstylist cutting hair in freezing gale-force wind, or an artist standing on a block of ice for eight hours while they sculpt - it wouldn't happen.

Set aside the technical difficulties of fluctuating conditions like wind, temperature and humidity, the interpersonal challenges of making coffee outside are immense. Try making meaningful conversation with a customer while your frozen hands struggle to gauge the milk temperature; try smiling genuinely when you're deeply uncomfortable; try staying in control of an incredibly temperamental product continuously throughout the day. To sum it up neatly: it takes immense fortitude to be a street coffee barista in London.

Complicating things further, a one-person street coffee operation is about as pure as you can do it. You're standing on the street at the mercy of the elements, toe-to-toe with your customers. There's no physical barrier separating you from them; there's no front of house or back of house, it's live theatre with no fourth wall. It's as if the audience is sitting on the stage with the performers, and the audience has us cornered with nowhere for us to catch our breath away from the spotlight.

If the street coffee barista is tired, hungover or just not feeling it, there's no *"hide me away on shots"*, there's no other colleagues to front the customer on behalf of the team. You're a solo artist performing live on stage with no back up musicians. When the lead singer of a band turns up to a gig stoned or strung-out, they know the string section will pick up the slack and mask over the cracks. Not here, not street coffee. Pumping out two hundred and fifty coffees on your own using a single group espresso machine is intense. Layer in customer rapport-building, queue politics, retail sales, re-stocking and endless cleaning – it's an act of multiskilling that would leave even the most capable multiskillers sucking their thumb and crying for mummy. So you can imagine the impact insomnia can have on a street coffee barista. It's beyond rough, it's torturous.

I was burning hotter and running harder than many people ever dare attempt. My mind and body were on high alert 24 hours a day, 7 days a week. I was balancing three very large things in my life – family man, International Marketing Director and small business Founder. One or two of these things would be enough for most people to attempt, I was doing all three at once. As a result the inevitable happened - that silent predator that'd been stalking me for months jumped out of the bushes and took me by the throat – I broke down and hit the ground hard. I was utterly beaten and exhausted beyond repair. But I had to get up and keep going, I had responsibilities to uphold.

If you've ever seen a boxing movie where the main character keeps getting off the canvas no matter how badly they're beaten – I felt like the coffee version of that, and my head was thumping with pain. But I kept getting off the canvas no matter how cold, tired, unwell, stressed or stretched I felt. People say true character is tested in moments of chaos; this was my version of chaos, and my true character was on full display to my family, friends, customers and digital audience. This is where my kids got to see what kind of man their dad really was. *Just keep going, Ant* is what I'd say to will myself into lacing up my shoes at 5.30am every morning. *Just keep going, it'll pass.* So that's what I did. Eventually the insomnia started to make way for short bursts of rest, followed by longer and longer periods of deep refreshing sleep.

In this borderline delusional state I had an epiphany. I wanted to start a brand conversation with our customers and digital audience that would set a differentiated, unique tone for Dear Coco. Something that didn't typically exist. This brand decision would set me and our small business apart from all others, and previously off-limits conversations around small business transparency would develop on a global scale. Without me realising, this decision would ultimately catch the attention of someone very powerful within the global business community that would change my life forever.

~~~~

Have you ever walked into a small business and thought: *"I wonder how much money they make?"* It's a natural curiosity to have. Wanting to quantify another's efforts and talent into one clean number to determine how they compare to us.

Being a small business owner is lonely. In the dead of night it can be a cocktail of anxiety, stress, worry and joy. Many owners don't have immediate colleagues or peers to openly share the journey. A professional network only exists if you diligently build and maintain one yourself. With only a small inner circle many business owners wrap a veil of secrecy around things like revenue, costs, net profit, debt and the like. The result being that small businesses don't tend to share their annual performance results like large businesses do. There's potential exposure to vulnerable feelings such as inadequacy or fear; there's the risk of being perceived as self-promoting or showboating. *What if people think I earn more than I actually do? What if my earnings don't match my efforts?*

Organisations at the shiny end of town share their annual results with shareholders and investors, they're obligated to. I'd worked within these organisations for the past thirteen years so I asked myself the question – *why shouldn't my own small business share the same level of detail with our community and customers if my intentions are true?* After all, our community and customers are the ones who drive all our success. Why shouldn't they know what they do for us if shared authentically? Personally, I'd love to know that my repeated custom was translating into success for a small, local business. Better yet, I'd be touched if they told me how they're doing.

So I made a significant brand decision for Dear Coco: I decided to buck the trend of small businesses globally and open our books for all to see. I share everything, warts and all, and nothing is off limits. I reveal our set-up costs; ongoing investments; cost of sales across all spend categories; total revenue; product profit margins; and the most secretive number of all – our net profit. I share our business milestones for the year and our digital performance. By now our followers see as much, if not more than Emma, my kids and our trusted accountant.

I told myself I needed to be at the forefront of the coffee industry if I'm going to make an impact. To be an industry leader I needed to add real, tangible value to people. I wanted to be an industry authority that people looked to for insights, best practice and advice. When you Google 'how to run a café' you'll see a thousand articles by a thousand different authors. If you Google 'how to run a coffee truck' I want to be the guy leading the conversation. But most significantly I don't hypothesise what cost of sales percentages and profit margins *should* look like – I show *actual* figures and stand proudly behind them. After three years of bringing our followers behind the curtain I'm able to give them a valuable year-on-year comparison, something that shows effort versus reward. We show growth of +16% between year two and year three, and what it took to get there.

Avid followers of Dear Coco send messages to say that our open-book approach to business provides the validation they need to invest in their own coffee truck dreams. I receive year-round messages from budding coffee entrepreneurs from Argentina, Indonesia, Mexico, America, South Africa, Australia, Romania, Croatia…the list is endless. I receive pictures and videos of newly built coffee trucks showing how we inspired their concept and design. Some businesses look so painfully close to the actual Dear Coco designs they're flirting with trademark infringements, but what do I care - these folks are living their dreams on the other side of the world to me. I'm so genuinely happy for them and this two-way dialogue makes me feel incredible, it makes me feel like I have colleagues and peers in this lonely occupation. I now feel valuable and recognised amongst my small business peers and coffee community.

But what's more difficult than getting to the forefront of an industry is staying there. *How can I keep creating such immense, tangible value with this tiny coffee truck that I become undeniable, inside and outside the coffee industry?* The impact created by this level of sharing made me feel important, and after three years of owning the narrative I felt like I'd done it – I'd become the global authority on how to own and operate a successful coffee truck business. No one is operating in this space the way I'm doing it, and the impact I'm having makes me feel invincible. I don't stop at sharing financial performance, I share every minute detail about the daily routine of being me – family man, International Marketing Director and small business founder. I bring people into my multi-faceted routine that's so disciplined and laced with unappealing grit it'd make David Goggins hide under his bed.

The team and I are the coffee version of a Bering Sea crab fisherman stepping out on deck when everyone else stays warm inside. No one wants my routine, but they're inspired by it because I'm a normal person just like them. People connect with regular people doing irregular things - if I'm a superhero or genetically gifted then I'm not relatable. People need to picture themselves within my routine and turn it down because it all feels too hard. They need to be physically able to do what I do, but decide to leave it to me and watch on with interest. I've become somewhat of a public motivational figure, and I have the coffee industry, small business community and families around the world cheering me on.

This all-access look inside Dear Coco's financial and operational performance stopped the coffee industry in its tracks. Industry commentators would speculate *"Why does this guy let us so deep inside his life and business? Why is he sharing this level of detail?"* This intrigue became Dear Coco's most unique proposition, and I was a credible source of information because I've shared everything from day one. This approach has created brand stickiness, loyalty and word of mouth promotion rarely enjoyed by such tiny businesses. It's made us successful beyond my wildest dreams, digitally and in real-life.

Allow me to share two Instagram posts that demonstrate the level of financial transparency our followers receive through my open-book approach to sharing:

Posted on Instagram, 30 December 2023

SPECIAL FEATURE: The Dear Coco 2023 Business Results. Have you ever walked into a small business and thought "I wonder how much money they make?" It's a natural curiosity to have. When I opened Dear Coco in 2021, I decided I'd operate an open-book business. You get to see everything, nothing's off limits. But why? Might you ask.

Big business releases its annual results to its shareholders & investors, it's obligated to. But why shouldn't a small business do the same for its community & customers…the people who drive our success. Why shouldn't you know what you do for us, we're nothing without you.

But there's another reason. Just because someone opens a business doesn't mean they've got it all figured out. Business ownership can be lonely. Owners look to each other as colleagues & peers. So if fellow owners find a learning, insight or a little self-validation from what I share, that's a good thing.

So enjoy this look inside Dear Coco's 2023 performance (scroll through the photos for our results). I hope it adds a little bit of value to you…whether you run a business, are interested in business, or just like being up in other people's business.

Yours in coffee,
Ant

Total Revenue: £168,233 (+16% versus 2022)
Trading 49 weeks, 5 days per week
Equivalent to USD $215K or AUD $314K or EUR €194K

Net Profit: £54,409 (32% of Total Revenue)
Equivalent to USD $70K or AUD $102K or EUR €63K
- This is the money our family receives from the business
- Net Profit for brick & mortar cafés is typically 5%-15%

Operating Costs: £113,824 (68% of Total Revenue)
- Wages (we pay London Head Barista rate): £35,964 (21.5%)
- Coffee (incl retails bags, oat milk, chocolate): £21,909 (13%)
- VAT Value Added Tax: £15,616 (9.5%)

- Bakes: £10,478 (6%)
- Miscellaneous Costs: £8,470 (5%)
- Repairs & Maintenance: £5,177 (3%)
- Milk: £4,005 (2.5%)
- Little Sweet Shop: £3,465 (2%)
- Disposables: £3,123 (2%)
- Payment Terminal Fees: £2,944 (1.75%)
- Utilities: £1,435 (1%)
- Rent (Street Trading Licence Fees): £1,231 (<1%)
- Marketing: Nil (0%)

Business Highlights

- Our debt level is zero.
- YoY growth of +16% was achieved trading one less week and doing fewer private events than 2022.

- Major Investments:
  - Replacement Linea Mini coffee machine: £4K
  - Failed expansion into brick & mortar (sad face): £6K
- Key Product Profit Margins:
  - Flat White (specialty coffee, double shot @ £3.30): 82%
  - Bakes: (@ £2.90): 60%
- Sales Split by Category:
  - Coffee: 84.7%
  - Bakes: 10.6%
  - Little Sweet Shop: 4.7%
- Milk Sales Split:
  - Dairy Milk: 75%
  - Oat Milk: 25%

- Most Popular Coffees:
  - Flat White: 32%
  - Latte: 22%
  - Cappuccino: 19%

Digital Highlights

- Instagram Update:
  - Followers: 16.8K (+116% in 12 months)
  - Top Countries: U.K, United States, Mexico, Australia, Indonesia.
  - Most popular post: 'Hidden coffee spot' in collaboration with @coffeeandbrunch 3.8M+ views, 140K engagements.
- LinkedIn Update:
  - Followers: 4K+
  - Most popular post: 'Credibility Stock Exchange' 4.5M+ views and 47K engagements.
- FLTR Magazine 1st and 3rd most popular feature articles of 2023
  - 'Street coffee truck to brick & mortar…then back again' by Anthony Duckworth
  - 'A step-by-step guide to creating a successful coffee truck business' by Anthony Duckworth

Posted on Instagram, 1 July 2024

SPECIAL FEATURE: Our 2024 Financial Results (1 January - 30 June). So why do I share our financial performance with you guys? There's a few reasons…

I want to enable other coffee truck entrepreneurs with information and validation. I want to lead from the front.

You guys own these numbers, without you they don't exist. I want to show you what you do for us, we're growing up together.

I'm deeply proud of our performance, our team and partners who deliver day in day out.

Seeing growth against the same period last year brings a tear to my eye. We had to close unexpectedly in February to return to Australia to say goodbye to my dad. We've still delivered revenue growth of +5% while trading 6 fewer days. My goodness that's incredible, especially given we grew 16% YoY in 2023.

THANK YOU for making this possible, I'm so humbled by all this.

Ant & Team

Dear Coco H1 2024 Financial Results		
	H1 2024 (GBP)	versus H1 2023
Total Revenue	£89,039	+5.9%
Total Costs	£58,389	+2.6%
Net Profit (GBP)	£30,650	+£3,445
Net Profit (% of Total Revenue)	34.4%	+2.1%
# Days Traded	134	6 fewer days
Net Profit is the amount Ant's family receives after all costs are paid		

Chapter 8
Street Coffee Confidential

From the age of thirteen or fourteen I was branded a 'natural storyteller'. At school I was terrible at maths and even worse at science, but hand me a blank notebook and a pencil and I soared. My favourite questions to receive at exam time were ones that encouraged me to express myself, be creative and go where I wanted to go. So, it stood to reason that once my school journey was complete, and I readied myself for university, I was considered one of the school's most gifted English writing students. I adored writing and still do, but to this day I remain entirely untrained in the art form.

Standing on the street as a solo barista is a lonely experience. Yes, we're surrounded by customers and passers-by all day, but most of the time those are quickfire, surface-level conversations lacking emotional depth due to the limited time available with each person. Many street baristas don't have colleagues or team-mates to share the daily eight-hour experience with, so there's limited opportunity to talk about what's on our mind or why we might be feeling sad, upset or happy.

For me, recounting tales from the truck by way of digital storytelling helps fill the hole created by such an isolated profession. This was a core reason I adopted a long-form content approach on Instagram – I need words to bring the reader right into the experience with me, not just show a pretty picture with a headline that gives them zero insight into what we're experiencing. Long-form, vulnerable stories that encourage our audience to slow down have been a core pillar of Dear Coco's media success. Our followers get a credible coffee feed to observe and enjoy, while also getting a seat at my digital dinner table to hear everything that goes on behind the shiny façade of the truck.

~~~~

In 2000 Anthony Bourdain took us inside the restaurant kitchen for a tell-all look at an intense, insular profession with brutal working hours, questionable conditions, terrible pay and everything in between. After three years within the coffee industry's toughest category, allow me to bring you inside the world of street coffee with Dear Coco's most notable, disturbing, raw short stories as told from the coffee truck. I hope you enjoy them.

Welcome to the Jungle

Let me be clear: I'm not the hardest working person around. There are people out there who do harder, longer, more meaningful work than me. I'm not a superhero nor do I need people to shout *"atta boy"* to keep me going or throw tickertape parades to celebrate my achievements. What I will say is my work schedule commands tenacity, a level of commitment and grit that many people simply refuse to take on. Everyone has their own reasons for not taking on as much as I do. Some prefer to focus deeply on family or alone time; some don't have the will power or outside interests; some aren't inspired to adopt a heavier life than the one they currently lead; and some are simply waiting for the lightning bolt to hit before they change their life.

I'm just a regular guy doing some irregular things. My superpower is pushing things forward with a level of commitment that's hard to find. Whether I'm relocating a family across the world, teaching English as a second language on the outskirts of Madrid, tending bar for £4.30 an hour while working full-time, or building a coffee truck business from scratch – fewer people will push harder than me. My rareness is my ability to live my version of a maximised life and endure hardship after hardship on the path to whatever success I can earn. Anyone can do what I do, most choose not to. With this spirit, welcome inside my daily routine of family man, International Marketing Director and small business founder:

- Up at 5.30am. Drink my (proverbial) can of cement and harden up! Receive the milk & bake deliveries. Slice & package the bakes. Get myself ready.
- 6.30am load the coffee truck.
- 6.50am drive the truck to the river.
- 7.00am arrive to the river. Write our social media post sitting in the truck. Take a deep breath before stepping out into the cold.
- 7.15am start the truck set up, our barista arrives at 7.30am.
- 8.00am we're open! Enjoy my owner's perk flat white, have a quick chat with some customers, leave for my corporate job in Belgravia, Central London.
- 8.45am my corporate day starts, including calls with Australia, Europe and the US.
- 6.30pm leave the office and return to the river.
- 7.30pm arrive to the river. Drive the truck home (in traffic).

- 8.00pm arrive home. Unload the truck, re-stock and clean the barista equipment.
- 8.45pm tuck Coco (the kid) into bed. Eat dinner.
- 9.30pm leadership meetings with New York.
- 10.00pm sit down with Emma and hang with Malia and Lani.
- 10.30pm bounce a few Slack messages around with my corporate team in Australia.
- 11.00pm bedtime.

It's a lot I know, but when you enjoy the process as much as the outcome (also known as money after being poor), the cement can taste like rosé! It should be noted, the above routine does not apply in its entirety on Mondays and Tuesdays when Dear Coco is closed. Those days do not require me to visit the river in the morning or evening, which provides welcome respite to ensure my professional routine is sustainable long-term.

Emma and I work as a team to not only create the space needed to achieve what I need to achieve, but also give our family and friends everything they need. Everyone and everything in my life gets my full, adoring attention. If it didn't I'd re-prioritise my life so it did. Dear Coco will never be the reason other parts of my life start to feel neglected, its designed to enhance my family's life, not compromise it. If this was to ever happen, I shit you not I would close the business overnight and walk away. Nothing is more important to me than Emma and my girls.

'No Dickheads'

I have one customer-facing policy at the truck. It's simple, clear and self-explanatory – No Dickheads.

Here's the thing, our coffee truck doesn't have a front door. Customers don't have to step over a threshold to engage with our business. We park up against the kerb on a public street with no physical separation between public land and private business. For this reason there can be a tendency for a (very) few socially challenged members of the general public to believe we're on their turf, and treat us however they see fit. Customers will almost never open the front door of a brick-and-mortar retail store, walk in, abuse the staff and walk out. It's just not socially acceptable or common behaviour amongst the vast majority of people. Why would you walk into someone else's premises and insult them? But what happens when there's no physical front door or invisible social construct to prevent this kind of behaviour, like at the Dear Coco coffee truck?

To protect my team from any outlandish, unfair behaviour being thrown at them I enacted the Dear Coco 'No Dickhead Policy'. This policy has been in place since day one and it's inked into the Standard Operating Procedure of our business, or at least it would be if we had one. But what does this policy mean and what does it do? It's quite simple really – if your behaviour towards our team is deemed dickhead standard then you're banned from the business, gone. There's no first or last warnings, there's no *"sorry Ant it won't happen again"*. You're done, see ya.

I can't provide any physical safety to my team standing in a public space with no front door to close on unruly customers, so I need to close the proverbial front door instead. Of course they can tell me to go to hell and ignore my instructions not to return, but very few people are built that way. Therefore the policy has worked well to date and we've had very few incidents that weren't easily solvable. Except for one.

It was a Saturday early afternoon and our barista and Lani were running the shift. It was an exceptionally busy morning and the team found themselves running short of dairy milk. For some reason that day we didn't have as many oat milk sales as normal, so our daily supply of fourteen two-litre bottles of whole milk was in danger of running out before the shift finished. Lani called to let me know, and luck was on our side that I was at home at the time of the call. I loaded the car with more milk, grabbed Coco and set off to the river.

When I arrived at the truck there was a long queue, so I loaded the milk bottles into the onboard fridge without disturbing the team, who were busy serving customers. I didn't want to distract the team so I took Coco's hand ready to head off to the nearby playground for a run around. As I started to leave our barista asked if they could fill me in on a situation that was quietly playing out without me noticing. They pointed out a gentleman that was standing adjacent to the truck along the river wall, uncomfortably staring at the team while muttering words I couldn't make out. He was dressed in army surplus clothing and had a large backpack with him – suggesting he was carrying his entire life's possessions. It was clear from his appearance and demeanour alone that he'd fallen on hard times and wasn't in a 100% coherent state.

Our barista mentioned the gentleman had spent his time in the coffee queue shouting to other customers and passers-by that the COVID-19 vaccine was dangerous, and everyone should be ashamed for knowingly killing children with their approval to have it administered. His rants not only made customers feel uncomfortable, but the Dear Coco team as well.

The team had no choice but to operate the business with this playing out right in front of them. They were pinned in position and had no way of moving away apart from closing the business down which neither of them wanted given the long queue of customers. My responsibility as founder is to protect the team at all costs and provide a fair, comfortable working environment for them to perform. This man had broken that happy bubble surrounding Dear Coco so I needed to step in and help.

I asked Coco to stay next to Lani and I approached the man while he was mid-rant, only a few metres away from the truck. I introduced myself as Ant, the owner of the coffee truck and asked if everything was OK. It was clear within seconds of starting the conversation this gentleman was not in a socially functional state. He had a level of rage across his face that instantly made me feel intimidated. I'm a gentle, slight, non-combative person by nature and suddenly I was in the firing line of someone who clearly wanted a fight. I was the poor sucker that took the bait. He zeroed in on me and he teed off. He began to insult me; tease my physical appearance; degrade my business; my kid and anything he could get his eyes on. He told me I looked like an arsehole in my knitted sweater and stood nose to nose with me like we were two professional fighters at the weigh in before the title fight. It got very heavy very fast. With Lani and Coco within arm's reach I immediately went into protector mode and started to behave in an overly combative, confrontational way that only inflamed the situation more.

After what felt like ten minutes of nose-to-nose abuse I couldn't take any more. Shamefully with Coco and Lani watching on I stood tall to this man and in my deepest, most combative voice I shouted *"Mate, fuck off. Get the fuck away from my business, get the fuck away from me. Fuck off and get some help"*. Coco got visibly upset seeing her dad in this state, and Lani as an impressionable thirteen-year-old was now seeing a side of dad she hadn't seen before. This was a big mistake on my part and I instantly regretted my approach. I'm usually better than this.

What I thought was aggressive behaviour previously had now erupted into a level of rage I'd not seen in front of me before. This man took things to a new level with obscenities which on their own didn't harm me, but what he said next was what truly worried me. He said he'll be coming back to the truck tomorrow and the coming days when I wasn't there to *"talk to your staff member"*. He threatened recurring visits to my business so he could intimidate (and for all I know, harm) the team. He looked me dead in my eyes and said I wasn't capable of dealing with the level of danger I had now attracted by telling him to fuck off. He said I'd given him all he needs to wreak havoc and fear on my business.

Oh boy, my team are now exposed and vulnerable to this man with no front door to keep the danger out. This was now a major problem. Through my own weakness and inability to weather a storm of insults, I'd inflamed a situation that was now dangerous for the team. The fire was out of control, I needed to pour cold water on the situation, fast. If he left without some kind of resolution I'd spend the next days/weeks/months waking up in fear, not knowing if today was the day he re-visited the truck and did something to a team member.

The only way to solve this was to hand him all the power and admit I was at fault. I calmed him down long enough to get some words in. I asked him to come over to the river wall slightly away from the truck so I could talk to him on a different level, with a different tone. I then told him it was all my fault – I told him I was wrong to fly off the handle; I'd told him to fuck off because I'd brought existing baggage into the conversation from a different situation earlier in the day – it was whatever I could do at that point. I told him I was wrong to talk to him like I did; I apologised and asked him to forgive me. It was a soul destroying, pride swallowing performance.

The mood changed instantly. He slowed his voice and his heartrate changed; he suddenly had all the power. He gave me a lecture on how he could physically bury me in seconds; how he could hurt me and my business at his whim; and that I wasn't physically built to deal with guys like him. I simply nodded and agreed with it all, I just needed to get this guy out of here with an agreement that he wouldn't return. After ten or so humbling, soul-crushing minutes of apologising to an irate junkie that he was right and I was wrong he said he appreciated me being *"a bigger man now"* and said he'd leave with no desire to return. I was shaking with relief.

I immediately needed to repair the damage I'd done with little Coco and Lani. They had not seen this kind of aggressive behaviour from me before and I needed to own my mistake. I apologised to them; I reinforced to Lani that I'd made a big mistake by inflaming a situation with even more aggression. I wanted to show her how to own a mistake, take accountability and be brave in the face of adversity by apologising for inappropriate behaviour. It didn't matter who was right and who was wrong, I wanted to be the stronger person in character, and apologising to an out-of-control addict felt like a lesson I was able to teach.

This man has never returned to the truck since.

12 Days

It was November 2023. The family was at home doing what families do to wind down from a busy day. Emma and I were doing bits and bobs around the house. Malia, like many fifteen-year-olds, was in her room scrolling through her phone. Coco was at her desk writing a list about what her teddy Big Bear does and doesn't like – apparently Big Bear loves cuddles and tickles, but doesn't like being left alone, too much sunlight or spit (I didn't realise Big Bear was exposed to a lot of spit, but it's good to know all the same!). Lani was on the sofa watching something on Netflix.

Then out of nowhere the calmness broke. It was as if someone flicked a switch. Within minutes of feeling absolutely fine, Lani started keeling over in excruciating pain saying it felt like someone was stabling her in the stomach with a knife. Emma and I ran through all the usual parent suggestions – have you eaten something funny? Do you need the bathroom? Would you like a hot water bottle and something for the pain? No matter what we did or what we offered Lani was in serious, gut churning pain that went on for hours.

Emma set up two makeshift beds in the living room so we could sleep in the same room and keep an eye on her. Lani normally sleeps on the top floor of our Victorian-style maisonette, but Emma wanted to monitor her throughout the night. Just as well too, as that night Lani vomited twenty two times in the space of eight-hours. The next morning Emma called 111 to ask for medical advice on what to do. Things felt dangerous, not to mention incredibly painful for Lani.

The medical advice was to take Lani immediately to Chelsea and Westminster Hospital and go straight to A&E. Emma was told this was very serious and they needed to hurry. At the time I was in my corporate office in Central London, so Emma gave me an update once they arrived at A&E. The doctors didn't know what was wrong with Lani so they admitted her to the ward and commenced tests to try and discover what was going on. Two days of tests, x-rays and ultrasounds revealed nothing, so she went for an MRI scan to get a definitive answer. A burst appendix was the diagnosis.

This in itself is not an uncommon occurrence, however the time it took the hospital to discover what happened meant that Lani had developed sepsis to the point where she was dangerously ill. Within the hour Lani was having the four hour procedure to remove her appendix and as much of the toxic pus that was infecting her insides as possible. We were told there was a 50% chance she'd need a second operation given the volume of toxic fluid sitting in her stomach, but we wouldn't know for certain for several days. As a result, Lani was not able to drink a drop of water or eat a morsel of food for ten days. Let me say that again: Lani was not able to drink a drop of water or eat a morsel of food for ten days! Her stomach needed to be completely empty in the event she needed a second operation. The doctors also needed to give her stomach time to stop producing horrible green bile that would have prevented her from keeping any food or water down anyway.

As human beings we all know there's a desperation that comes with hunger and thirst – so much so humans have been found eating other humans when desperate enough. So you can imagine the level of desperation this hunger and thirst created for poor Lani. It was utterly heart-breaking to deny her food and water when she was virtually crawling out of bed, pulling on the dozens of tubes coming in and out of her body to get to water. The doctor told us the human body can last eleven days without food or water before it starts to rapidly deteriorate – Lani got to ten days before they let her sip some water and eat tiny pieces of food. This inspiring young lady was incredible in strength and resolve to live with this form of torture for so long. Our family remains deeply proud of how she handled this incredibly difficult time.

Lani was housed in the Intensive Care Unit at Chelsea and Westminster Hospital and placed on morphine. She was in charge of self-administering her morphine round the clock whenever she felt the pain levels were unbearable. This meant that once the dosing machine surpassed the allowed time to re-administer doses (I recall this being 5-10 minutes), Lani would press the button, over and over. Seeing your child so heavily dosed on such strong pain medication is an upsetting sight. Lani's eyes were rolling back in her head, and she had a lack of coherence that resembled someone who had overdosed on drugs at some house party. It's extremely difficult to watch let alone encourage her to keep pressing the button to ease the pain.

As a parent you fear your child becoming addicted to any substance they associate with making them feel better – so Emma and I hoped this period wouldn't leave a lasting appetite to lean on drugs to deal with challenges after she'd left hospital. You hear of people getting addicted to pain medication all the time, so this was a genuine worry for Emma and me.

The next twelve days were spent sitting by Lani's hospital bed in intensive care. She was almost never left alone, and Emma was herculean in her love and support for Lani. Out of the twelve nights in hospital, Emma slept on a rickety old foldout cot for eight of them, and I did the other four nights to give her a much-needed break. Emma was suffering from a bad back and problematic shoulder at the time, so sleeping on such an unstable surface was utter torture for her. But anyone who knows Emma will agree, she's as strong in mind and spirit as anyone. No one would know the discomfort she was enduring.

Anyone who's tried sleeping in a hospital room will tell you the same thing – sleep is impossible. Whether you have your own room or, like us, you're sharing with three other patients and their families – it's an incredibly loud, busy environment. And so it should be, it's a hospital not a hotel. Every minute is filled with beeps, buzzers, alarms, nurse visits, doctor visits, patients screaming in pain, carers and families screaming in frustration. It's a lot. The reality is no one except those on morphine get any sleep while in hospital. So on top of the always-on worry about Lani's condition, the fatigue and sleep deprivation Emma and I were experiencing was intense.

The decision around what to do with Dear Coco over this period was a very difficult one. I had already confirmed our operating hours with our barista team for the next ten days, so it was my responsibility to ensure they had paid work for this entire time. Closing the business for ten days while continuing to pay their wages was not a viable option, and there wasn't enough annual leave accrued for the team to redeem. It was on me to figure this out, and the only solution was to open the business as normal.

Somehow I needed to figure out how to drop the truck in position each day, perform my corporate day, pick up the truck at night, do my evening owner's responsibilities, be a dad and a supportive husband and for four nights make all this happen while also sleeping at the hospital. To say it was a daunting task would be a serious understatement. This routine would require strength and will power rarely called upon. Emma and I were trying to run a family of five, a corporate career and two small businesses (Emma owns and operates *www.emmaduckworthbakes.com* where she creates and shares recipes for the at-home baker. She is also a food photographer and published author of her own cookbook *Simply Sweet Nostalgic Bakes*), plus caring for our other two children while losing one of us full-time to hospital duties. It's not lost on me that many families around the world face the same challenges, and more. This was not a unique situation to us and we were advantaged by the fact that Emma and I have a strong partnership. Others have to do it alone.

On the nights I slept at the hospital I would sneak out of Lani's room at 3.30am, return home to collect the truck, drive it to the river and do the morning set up so the business was ready for our barista. By 5.30am I would be back in Lani's hospital room before she even knew I was gone. I would either work my corporate day from Lani's bedside or Emma would take over and I'd work from home. At 9.30pm I'd return to the river to collect the truck and bring it home to commence the evening re-set routine. I would be in bed by midnight, and up again at 3.30am to repeat the routine. This went on for twelve days and the impact was immense.

As Lani recovered in hospital, Emma and I were learning just how far it's possible to push the human spirit. We were truly and utterly exhausted, but when there's only one option you simply have to commit to it and endure the consequences. So that's what we did and as a result Lani felt loved and cared for the entire time, Malia and Coco always had a parent or family friends providing all they needed and Emma and I showed what a strong, loving marriage we have.

The far easier path would have been to close Dear Coco for twelve-days, pay the £1,500 wage bill and wear the financial loss. Not only was this not palatable given our customers would have also felt this impact (although every single one of them would have understood completely) – this was my opportunity to practice what I preach. I tell people I'm a regular guy doing irregular things, this was my opportunity to show it once again.

I used these twelve days to show my girls what exceptional commitment can look like. I was available and committed to everyone who needed me, I lived up to all my responsibilities, I put the right people in the right places to deliver on the right things. We leaned on friends for help and my corporate team supported me at work, we covered all bases and made sure Malia and Coco's lives were as normal as possible. If true character is tested in moments of chaos, I give myself and Emma an A+ for this test.

An Instagram post I published on 15 November 2023, when we finally got back from hospital, neatly captures what those twelve days felt like for the family:

A mother falls asleep upright in a hospital room. During the day she alternates between hospital & home keeping a family of five afloat. Her client work is piling up.

A father loads a coffee truck at 4.30am. He does 15-hour workdays, many from his daughter's bedside. At 9.30pm he collects the truck and resets for the next day. He gets 4 hours sleep most nights.

A 15-year-old misses her sibling, worrying she might need more surgery. She sits her mock GCSE exams with all this going on. She can't hear mum & dad cheering her on.

A 7-year-old gets passed around from house to house, before & after school. Her parents can't possibly be everywhere. She longs to be picked up from school by mum. She has tears in her eyes most nights.

The last 12 days have demanded a level of strength & determination rarely called upon in many people's lives, including our own.

Our daughter is now out of hospital. She endured 12 days in intensive care after a burst appendix and sepsis. She couldn't eat for 12 days, can you imagine what that feels like! She will now spend the next couple of weeks recovering at home. We feel deeply happy she's out.

When you break a bone it heals stronger than its original

condition. Emma & I were taken to breaking point, as was our daughter. But the power of our marriage & friendship meant we never broke. The strain will make us stronger than our original condition, if that's even possible.

We're deeply grateful to our friends, colleagues & team members for giving us the space we needed to endure. Our love goes to the families that don't make it out of there whole. We're the lucky ones. Now, we heal.

Wet Socks and Dirty Fingernails

With many professions and endeavours there can be a disconnect between perception and reality. Social media (or should I say, the users within it) do a great job of giving the impression everything's hunky dory. Most brands apply a shiny, customer-facing veneer that shelters their followership from seeing what's truly going on behind the scenes.

In line with my all-access, transparent approach to operating Dear Coco, I've not only never hidden the challenges and struggles of running a coffee truck, but I've used them as headlines. People connect most deeply with real people facing real-world challenges, ones they'll likely face themselves in one form or another. We've all been caught in the rain, experienced power issues, property flooding or scrambled to be somewhere on time after an unexpectedly chaotic morning. These are things that almost everyone can relate to, so why hide things away that will likely create a deeper, more emotional connection to your business?

A relatable challenge I continuously face operating Dear Coco alongside a professional marketing career are early morning curveballs having a knock-on effect with the rest of my day. When Mother Nature's your landlady, as is the case with Dear Coco being an outdoor business, you have to be prepared to face issues outside your control. Every business experiences curveballs, however I'll suggest not as many as a 100% outdoor business that doesn't have walls, doors or a ceiling to keep the elements at bay.

A common issue I face doing business along the hallowed turf of Strand on the Green is street flooding. Strand on the Green is a flat street that runs alongside the River Thames, which in itself is susceptible to king-sized tides and flooding. To compound the issue, there aren't enough drains along the street to handle the volume of water heaped upon them, and the drain covers easily become blocked with leaves falling from the trees lining the street.

It's not uncommon for me to arrive in the truck at 7.00am to find our pitch completely underwater. Water can gather at a depth that makes parking and operating almost impossible without a snorkel and wetsuit. When this happens I open my second can of cement for the day, take a few deep breaths and deal with the issue as quickly as possible so as not to delay our 8.00am opening and my departure towards my corporate workday.

One particular morning sticks in my memory as a true demonstration of perception versus reality. It was September 2023 and months earlier I was faced with a business decision. The week commencing 18 September was going to be my busiest week of the year for my corporate marketing job. My European team was delivering a large, complex, high profile multi-day event for my organisation's most important global clients. Everyone was flying into London to attend this event; we had our most important senior clients arriving from all over Europe; we had the executive team from my organisation attending from New York and across Europe; we had media figureheads, global business leaders and celebrities attending and speaking. To put it mildly, this event was my team's most important project of the year so it had to be planned and executed to perfection.

True to form, I considered what that week should look like for Dear Coco given I'd be heavily relied upon in Central London for this major event. I assessed what impact this commitment would have on my team; our customers; our financial ambitions; and on me as the guy who had to glue it all together. My now well-known ironclad resolve to deliver on my promises couldn't have it any other way – Dear Coco would be open as usual throughout this chaotic period, and it was on me to figure out how to do it responsibly.

Day one of the event happened without a hitch. I dropped the truck in position early in the morning, made my way to Hotel Café Royal just off Regent Street and delivered an outstanding experience in partnership with my team, agency partners and business stakeholders.

Day two rolled around and I had the well-oiled 'Ant machine' humming. After getting home at midnight the night before, the truck got dropped into position along the river at 6.00am. I set everything up so our barista didn't need to do it all herself and I headed off to Regent Street to deliver another exceptional day. We then adjourned the group to a stunning dinner event at Somerset House. I told myself this was all working like clockwork, I was delivering on every promise I'd made across my corporate and small business worlds. Yes, I was getting zero sleep, but the energy flowing through my body kept me going.

On the way home from dinner at Somerset House the heavens opened, dumping a large volume of water onto Central London. My taxi was driving through lakes of water so deep I wondered if the car was going to hydroplane across the Embankment. Given my general tiredness in this moment I didn't put two and two together that this might impact the state of Strand on the Green in the morning. I just closed my eyes and allowed the driver to get me to the truck so I could take it home and prepare for the next day's trade. Arriving at the truck the weather was bad, but not as chaotic as I had just driven through in Central London, so off home I went to start the late night re-set procedure.

Day three arrived – the final day of this crazy event. After another night of three hours' sleep I was feeling the pinch physically. Now on the home stretch, I willed myself to keep pushing, telling myself I was doing great. Once again I followed the same routine – I showered and got into business attire suitable for such a prestigious event, although being the final day we allowed ourselves a slightly more casual dress code which included tailored jeans instead of suit pants. I skipped breakfast (against the constant advice I give to my girls) and headed off in the truck towards the river.

Driving up Chiswick High Road, round Gunnersbury roundabout and turning left onto Strand on the Green, it started to become clear that last night's weather pattern had wreaked havoc on Chiswick while I slept. The roads had a level of debris covering them like a named hurricane had just swept through town. Every single street drain was blocked, resulting in gigantic puddles of water cutting across every major and secondary road. When I turned onto Strand on the Green and rounded the gentle left sweeping turn leading away from Kew Bridge the reality of what this weather system had done became painfully clear. Drains that struggled to disperse far more modest volumes of water had buckled under the pressure. The cursory amount of water that often shallow flooded our pitch was now a fully-fledged lake that deserved its own name, Google location and souvenir guy selling cheap keychains to visitors. This new 'lake' was deep, long and wide!

I found myself muttering *"strewth"* (a softer Aussie slang word when saying 'f^*k' isn't appropriate, sorry kids). I was sitting in the idling coffee truck ten metres away from the new and very unattractive 'Lake Coco'; I was dressed in full business attire softened by tailored jeans; it was day three of my biggest project of the year; and to compound the panic I needed to get to Hotel Café Royal early that morning to meet and greet our headline guest, Steven Bartlett.

Steven is a British-Nigerian Entrepreneur, Founder, Investor and Host of the *Diary of a CEO* podcast, named Top 10 global podcast in 2023. Steven is an exceptionally in-demand, busy man. For a guy who publicly says he doesn't work before 11.00am I was beyond honoured that he accepted our invitation to the event. I needed to ensure I arrived at the hotel before he did.

As I saw it I had two choices. Option one - lock up the truck on the banks of the new 'Lake Coco', cut my loses and jump in a taxi towards Regent Street. Or, option two

– solve the issue, fulfil all my commitments and show my girls no amount of adversity can ever break their dad. I chose option two, of course I did.

It was time to get to work. I took off my humbly priced but beautifully stylish Zara suit jacket, removed my shoes and socks and waded through water that was halfway up my shins. I submerged my hands into the freezing cold water trying to find the two drain covers that had been covered over by thick mud, leaves and sticks during the storm. After who knows how many minutes of fumbling around underwater to find the drains I found the metal grate covers. I clawed my fingernails through the compacted mud and leaves, throwing armfuls of soggy debris towards the river wall so I didn't make a mess of the footpath. Once I cleared enough muck I saw the water vortex starting to form and the water started subsiding. Given the volume of mud and leaves heading towards the drains in the flowing torrent I needed to spend another ten-minutes running between the two drains continually clearing new debris so the water could continue to flow. If I was to stop myself in that moment and wonder what aliens would think of what they were witnessing along Strand on the Green, Planet Earth – I suspect they'd assume *Candid Camera* was relaunching and this was the first episode. It would have been comical to watch I'm sure.

Ten minutes passed and the water subsided enough to now park the truck in position, and it was time for another decision. Option one – set up the truck before leaving so the barista didn't have to do the entire routine themselves, which in my mind wasn't a demonstration of sound leadership. Or, option two – leave the truck in an incomplete state and make my way into the city knowing

I was already thirty-minutes behind schedule. I chose option one (of course I did) and spent the next thirty-minutes setting up the truck before leaving knowing I had owned the problem and didn't pass it onto our barista.

I was now sixty minutes behind schedule; I had frozen hands and feet; wet socks after getting re-dressed; and large clumps of dirt under my fingernails from clawing my way through mud to disperse 'Lake Coco'. I checked the Uber app and for some reason they couldn't locate me a driver, so I set off on foot towards Gunnersbury Tube Station, a ten minute walk or a five minute run. I decided to run given my predicament, and anyone who knows me will know that Ant doesn't run!

At this point my business attire was looking like a fancy dress costume I'd purchased from a charity shop on my way to a Bucks Night. My hands and dirty fingernails looked like I could be a suspect in a woodland disappearance case. I arrived at Gunnersbury Station only to see a mortifyingly messy, inconsiderate-to-my-circumstances handwritten sign stating that due to heavy rainfall there were no trains running from this station. This now explained why the Uber app couldn't match me with a driver. Everyone was screwed.

Strewth, what to do? Run, and remember Ant doesn't run! I set off on (wet) foot and ran towards Chiswick Park, the next accessible station that wasn't impacted by the heavy rain. This station was just under one kilometre away but it was the only option left, so away I went. By the time I got onto a train at Chiswick Park I was late, really late. I only had until Gloucester Road to place enough phone calls and text messages to my onsite events team to brace for my delayed arrival before my train went out of cell phone reception. As I made the arrangements, my fellow train passengers literally held their loves ones close while notifying Transport for London there was an unusual man on the District Line who looked like he was on the run from the police – I looked terrible.

I arrived at the Hotel Café Royal very late. I spent five minutes getting my appearance in order in the hotel lobby bathroom, which thankfully had soft linen towels, cologne and toiletries. I then arrived on level two of the five-star hotel looking like I'd just stepped out of a magazine shoot. I was smooth, well put together, eloquent and smelled amazing. Moments later four members of Steven Bartlett's personal team arrived into the room, followed by the man himself. As my heart rate continued to slow from the scramble that ended only moments earlier I shook Steven's hand with wet socks and so much dirt under my fingernails I talked with my hands in my pockets the entire time.

What I achieved that day was immense. I owned all my responsibilities; assumed accountability; demonstrated courageous leadership and rallied the right people at the right times to ensure business continuity. Most importantly I demonstrated to my girls, my team and the Dear Coco followers that no matter how insurmountable a situation might feel, I'll always act with integrity and never take the easy way out.

Whether I'm hosting clients at Wimbledon, flying to Sydney on business or attending leadership meetings in New York – I will always deliver on the promises I've made no matter how hard or disruptive they feel. I only commit to closing the business two or three weeks a year to create space for my international work commitments and a family holiday, but outside that no situation or circumstance will ever break my determination to open the business and deliver.

When it Rains, it Pours

Whether you run a business or run a household, equipment failure, maintenance issues and breakages are a fact of life. For high-traffic businesses like cafés and coffee trucks the equipment takes a serious beating. We interact with tens of thousands of customers a year and countless hours of baristas and adverse weather conditions that push the infrastructure to its limits. So it stands to reason things will break or go wrong at some point.

Putting fragile, sensitive, expensive coffee making equipment inside a moving vehicle is fraught with risk. When you have a £5,000 espresso machine sitting next to a £2,000 grinder being powered by a £4,000 onboard generator, the risks are immense. When driving the truck to and from our location I need to avoid every pothole in the road. If I hit a pothole that's over a certain depth it's almost certain the sensitive machinery in the back will be damaged. All it takes is a broken solenoid, damaged connection or snapped wire and the business will grind to an instant halt (pun intended and achieved). Therefore I have to treat the truck and the equipment housed within it with great care.

This is one of the main reasons why I maintain the personal responsibility of delivering the truck to the river each morning and returning it home at night. Yes, this is a great way for me to stay on the front lines of the business and connect to the team and customers – but ensuring the truck and equipment are handled with white cotton gloves is vitally important.

As you know, when I designed and built the truck in early 2021, I went to great expense to have a state-of-the-art petrol generator installed. I invested £4,000 on a Hyundai generator typically used to power large motorhomes, and the build team achieved an engineering feat by concealing and soundproofing the generator to a market-leading standard.

The problem with this approach was when the generator broke down it needed open-heart surgery, requiring the truck to be returned to the factory where it was built – four hours north of London on the back of a transport truck at great cost and impact to the business. Sadly, one only learns some lessons after decisions have already been made, and this reality would create the biggest single issue I'd face in the history of the business up until that moment.

Throughout the first six months of trading we had some minor issues with our generator. These issues were nothing a local mechanic couldn't address with some lateral thinking and a ridiculous wage bill for the inordinate amount of time each repair took. I was reasonably happy with the power solution, but it constantly bothered me that the customer and barista could hear more than a gentle hum of the generator, and it would pulse whenever power was being drawn.

The holy grail of power for coffee trucks is access to mains power. With our pitch positioned on the side of the road along the river, we may as well have been in the Australian Outback as far as mains power was concerned. I therefore persisted with the generator, and even amongst these noise and smell inconveniences it felt like our only reasonable power option. Then one day everything changed. It was a Friday and I was making a customer their coffee. Without warning the truck's entire electrical system started to fade on and off, and the espresso machine began to struggle. The generator started making horrible grinding, pulsing sounds before CLUNK! The entire truck operation went dark, it was dead as disco.

There was nothing I could do but close the business immediately and race the truck five-minutes up the road to the local mechanic who worked on the generator previously. He very kindly created space in his workshop so he could diagnose the problem right away. For three-hours he conducted surgery on the difficult-to-access generator only to say it was unrepairable and it needed to be returned to Hyundai for a full replacement given it was still within warranty.

This was a disaster. The only way for me to get this generator out of the truck is to transport the Piaggio four hours north of London via a transportation company at a return cost of approximately £1,000. The generator would then be removed from the truck and sent to Hyundai HQ, who would take as long as they needed to do their own diagnosis and either repair it or provide a replacement. Anyone who's been involved in a warranty claim before will know nothing ever moves fast, so it might be weeks or even months before the truck build team received a new generator to re-install and return the truck to London. I was well and truly stuck. My lateral thinking brain went into overdrive wondering how I could not only fix the generator, but keep trading with no access to power.

My first problem-solving phone call was to a man named Jon, the General Manager of the pub directly opposite our pitch on Strand on the Green. From the moment we rolled up to trade along the river Jon was the first to extend his hand in welcome. Many perceived Dear Coco as a direct competitor to Jon's pub given he also served take away coffee from the bar. But I'm sure Jon would acknowledge that coffee was not a core offering for the pub so he was gracious in treating me as a non-threatening friend. Jon went so far as to consider Dear Coco good for business given we were a beautiful addition to the local area, which in turn increased foot traffic for all other local businesses to enjoy. Jon is a friend, and on this occasion he needed to be my saviour.

I called Jon and asked if we could meet around the corner from his pub for an urgent chat and told him Dear Coco was in trouble. Immediately after we met I came out with the request that I'm sure we were both thinking in that moment, *"Jon, can I run power from your pub across the road to the truck for a few weeks?"* Before I could even finish my sentence Jon agreed, and in that moment he became the first ever Dear Coco saviour. Now we needed to make it happen.

Although the plan was simple in principle it took some choreography to activate. First, I needed to purchase a closed cable track that satisfied all local and national health and safety requirements to run across a road utilised by cars, heavy trucks, bikes and pedestrians. Secondly, Jon would need to brief his management team to feed a dedicated power board under the pub's front door before they locked up for the night. I'd then arrive in the morning and plug my cable that was running across the road (housed within the cable track) into the power board.

Next, we needed to hope and pray that no one would trip over the cable track and do themselves an injury. And lastly, we needed to hope Jon's boss, the Regional Manager of the national pub group didn't stop by during Dear Coco's trading hours and see us drawing power from his pub at no charge. Lots needed to go right, but Jon's pub was the only accessible building to draw power from so I needed to make it work.

Day one of our new power arrangement arrived and I was unbelievably nervous about how it would work. I arrived at the river at 6.30am, a little earlier than normal, to give myself extra time to get used to our new routine. I parked the truck, unrolled our new rubber cable track and laid my power cord inside. I waited for a break in whatever light traffic was passing at such an early hour and ran the cable track directly across the road from the truck to outside the pub's front door. All that was left to do was plug my power cable into the power board left underneath the pub's front door by the pub supervisor the previous evening. But there was a major problem – there was no power board to plug into! Jon's supervisor had forgotten to put it out before leaving for the night. Oh brother.

With no other option available I reluctantly and sheepishly called Jon on his mobile phone. It was 6.45am, an utterly unfair time to call someone who worked ridiculously long hours and treated sleep like a rare commodity. Unbelievably Jon answered, his phone voice clearly indicating he'd only had one or two-hours sleep. He was not due into work that day and had been out the night before with friends.

I told Jon my predicament. Instead of saying *"Mate, we'll have to deal with it later",* or *"Just write off today and we'll start again tomorrow"*, Jon got out of bed, got dressed, jumped on his motorcycle and came down to the river to open the pub and fetch the power board. Over the course of many months this happened over a dozen times, and not once did Jon refuse to help or complain. He simply wanted to do whatever he could to help a mate and see a small business succeed. Jon will stick in my mind forever for his generosity of spirit and friendship in my time of absolute need. And needless to say, he never paid for a coffee at Dear Coco again.

Assuming everything went to plan, I now had a semi-reliable source of mains power to allow me time to think of a longer-term solution. That solution would entail chasing the Holy Grail for coffee trucks – our own mains power installed at our pitch in partnership with the local council. What followed was a process and subsequent feeling not dissimilar to the loss and helplessness I experienced when dealing with the UK Visa and Immigration Office a few years earlier. Hounslow Council and the Local Planning Office did have an existing process established to deal with my power installation request, but nothing happened in a logical or timely manner.

Firstly, I needed planning permission – yes, the same permission required when building a house or block of flats. All I needed was a simple street furniture cabinet with a feeder pillar enclosed to tap into the mains power under the footpath, but the planning process was the same no matter the project size. After weeks and weeks of navigating a level of bureaucracy which I'm sure is designed to deter as many applicants as possible, I lodged the planning application. If successful, I would receive my approval to install mains power in five to six weeks. Once

I had the approval I would then need to work with Hounslow Highways to excavate the footpath to access the main supply powering the street. I'd then need SSE Energy Services to install the street cabinet and tap into the mains power underground. British Gas would then be needed to install a power meter inside the cabinet. And finally, a local electrician would be needed to install the power socket and fuse board inside the cabinet. It was an excruciating amount of work and number of suppliers for what is essentially a simple power socket inside a small metal cabinet, but remember, we're installing power outside a building or physical address, which adds untold complexity.

The cost for all these services would equal £6,000, a large investment for our tiny business, but a worthy one given it would provide stable, silent, long-term power. I informed Jon of the timeframes and he agreed to keep the arrangement of running power across the street going until I had our mains power installed.

Weeks later I was at home with Coco and I got a call from our barista who was working the shift that day. It was a sunny Saturday so there was lots of foot and road traffic along Strand on the Green. The barista told me there had been an accident – a man had ridden a small push scooter over our rubber cable track running across the road. He'd fallen forward and hit his face on the ground. I was mortified and couldn't get information fast enough as to whether the man was okay. I was told he broke his sunglasses, damaged his face and was (rightly) furious. I was given the man's number and I called him right away.

As expected, the conversation didn't go well. The man accused me of breaking the law by running a cable track across such a highly trafficked road, and I had created a public danger that caused him injury and distress. I told him the cable track I purchased satisfied all local and national health and safety requirements, and the only requirement stated in the Street Trading Policy was I couldn't lay 'exposed cables with the potential to cause a trip hazard'. In my mind by concealing the cables in an approved cable track I'd satisfied all my obligations, but he insisted I hadn't. It turned out this man was a retired judge, so was well positioned to recite the various laws I'd broken in my endeavours to keep powering my business. It was an intimidating and uncomfortable conversation, ending with the man saying he wouldn't report the issue to the council or police as long as I replaced his very expensive sunglasses. Of course I immediately reimbursed the man by bank transfer, but I did have question marks around whether what I'd done was indeed illegal. Equally confusing to me was why a grown man would knowingly ride a small push scooter over a highly visible cable track clearly too bulky to successfully cross with such tiny wheels. However I took responsibility, admitted fault and put it to bed. Or so I thought.

The following Friday I received a visit from a representative from Hounslow Council saying a formal complaint had been made about power being run across the road. I was immediately informed this arrangement could no longer continue despite my best efforts to rationalise the 'exposed cables' wording in the Street Trading Policy. It turned out new sunglasses and a verbal agreement weren't enough for this man to honour his own promise that the matter wouldn't go any further.

As of that moment our business was closed, and we had no more options to explore other than wait for our own mains power installation to be completed, which was still months away. Once again courage under fire and deep lateral thinking were required to solve this immense problem. As of this moment I was out of business; I had staff to pay and customers to keep engaged. We had generated enviable momentum since opening and had the eyes of the coffee world on us. We couldn't stop now. The only option in my mind was to find an alternative pitch with access to mains power that would let us trade for a couple of months while we waited for our power along Strand on the Green. Not only that, the pitch needed to be on private land as I didn't have the time required to apply for a new licence elsewhere. The only thing to do was walk miles and miles along the river searching for locations on private land with access to mains power and enough footfall to sustain a coffee truck needing to sell 150+ cups per day. This wouldn't be an easy task.

I spent the next day walking East along the river from Strand on the Green towards Hammersmith Bridge. It's a seven-kilometre stretch of river so surely there'd be multiple spots that suit these criteria, right? Wrong. For various prohibitive reasons there was only one spot that was suitable – the forecourt of Linden House, a beautifully converted riverside estate which hosted weddings, private events and the local rowing club. The forecourt was on private land, it directly fronted the Thames Path and had access to mains power down the staircase near the entrance to the changing rooms. It was like I'd struck gold. This needed to be our new home away from home. This was our only option.

I nervously approached the front door to Linden House, rang the intercom and asked to speak to the Venue Manager. She introduced herself and invited me upstairs for a chat. There I sat introducing myself as a local coffee truck founder that was down on his luck looking for a temporary home for his business. I showed her our burgeoning Instagram followership and cute pictures of Coco and I alongside the truck for emotional impact. I insisted if she let us trade outside we'd be a draw card to attract passers-by into the venue's forecourt, hence generating valuable exposure for her venue. Together with Jon from the pub, Dear Coco was then blessed to now have two saviours – I was granted immediate approval to trade outside Linden House. The next day I set up the truck, redirected our barista to our new location and spent the next two months trading along the river at Hammersmith while overseeing the deeply frustrating process of having power installed at our permanent location.

Instead of generating our usual £800-£900 daily sales, our new location was delivering £400-£500 a day. This was due to lower local awareness of our business and more sporadic footfall, but I was able to pay the bills and keep the team working with this revenue. Some regulars even walked the two hour round trip to Hammersmith and back, just to show their support for Dear Coco while we were 'away at camp'. The local Strand on the Green community deeply missed us, and their endless requests for updates on social media made us feel loved and valued.

This five month period was difficult for us as a business. It tested the commitment of our customers and demanded a steely resolve from me as founder and conductor of the multiple processes happening concurrently. Similar to when Lani was in intensive care, the option to close the business and re-build once the chaos had subsided was tempting, but that wouldn't have reflected my commitment to deliver for my team, my family and the people who were supporting our mission to survive. So we endured and were ultimately successful.

Super Bowl Week

I could see this week coming six months out; my busiest, most demanding week of the year. A week that made me want to crawl under my bed and hide. These seven days would take everything I had and push my mental and physical fortitude to new levels. Athletes spend weeks building up to their marquee week of the year where their life stops, senses are heightened and they need to perform at their optimum level – they refer to it as their 'Super Bowl Week'. This week was my Super Bowl Week and I was nervous about the impact it would have on me.

I'm incredibly selective and intentional about which private event bookings I accept for Dear Coco. Event bookings are a great way to expand our offering, generate new revenue streams and make profitable returns if the deal is right. However I *'decline with thanks'* 90% of the event enquiries we receive for a variety of reasons – the event location; event type; event purpose; budget available, etc. The main reason however is that our core focus and reason for being is street coffee. We heavily prioritise our street coffee customers because they're our lifeline, they're the ones who have made us so successful. For this reason I only commit to three or four private event bookings a year.

Two years earlier, a Saturday night in September 2021, I received a phone call as I was unpacking the coffee truck at home. It was a random guy who spotted me driving down Chiswick High Road only moments earlier. This man had a mate who worked for a guy who just had his coffee truck cancel on him due to the entire barista team contracting COVID-19. He urgently needed a truck at some event the following day, Sunday. I never take event bookings on a Sunday, it's our marquee trading day along the river where we get the most customers and most revenue. But I sensed the desperation and wanted to help if I could.

It turned out the event was *Concours of Elegance*, the world's most prestigious rare car show. If you're familiar with other famous British events such as *Royal Ascot* for horse racing or *Wimbledon* for tennis, the London *Concours of Elegance* is the equivalent event for rare cars. It's a very big deal that takes over the famed Hampton Court Palace grounds for three beautiful, uniquely British days every September.

I told the person on the phone that I'm a one-person coffee operation. I said I'm not prepared for an event tomorrow with staff or stock, but I'd give it a go with these caveats – I really wanted to help him out. We shook digital hands and the rest of the night was ladened with phone calls from the event operations team and security personnel onboarding Dear Coco as a new supplier for the event. I stayed up late that night getting my equipment and stock in order. I felt like a fighter getting ready for a big match. Given the timings I couldn't place any new stock orders, so I crammed every available crevice inside the truck with anything I could sell to ensure I made as much money as I would have along the river.

The next day I arrived at the event in my little truck only to then fully appreciate what I'd signed up for. The onsite security team came up and shook my hand wishing me good luck for what will be a momentous day for our tiny business. When multiple people say *"I hope you've eaten your Wheaties this morning!"* you know you're in for a big day. They made me feel like I was about to enter the Gladiator cauldron. That day I worked as hard as I've ever worked in my life. I made £1,200 worth of coffee and bake sales as a solo barista on a single group coffee machine – trust me when I say that's a LOT! Our existing one-day sales record along the river with a barista and assistant was £1,006, so you can imagine what this effort felt like working alone.

My work ethic in 2021 earned me so much street cred that in 2022 I was asked to return for the full three-day event. Then in 2023 we not only returned, but Dear Coco became the flagship coffee provider for the entire event. We were contracted to provide three separate on-site coffee activations – our truck in the general area, plus two private coffee enclosures for the world's most prestigious car company and a leading financial services organisation that sponsored the event. The expansion of Dear Coco's presence at this world-class event shows that sometimes one random phone call and a give-it-a-go attitude can change everything.

Dear Coco was now the flagship coffee provider for an event that attracts thousands of Europe's wealthiest and most adoring rare car lovers. The stakes were high; senses were heightened, and our performance needed meticulous planning and exceptional delivery – hence the Super Bowl Week nature of the week.

To fully appreciate the scale of my Super Bowl Week, here's the 30,000-foot view of how it was structured:

- Monday (UK Bank Holiday) – truck open along the river. Event & travel preparations. Collect truck at night, return home and restock.
- Tuesday – truck closed. Twelve-hour day at my corporate job. Home at 8.00pm.
- Wednesday – truck open along the river. Ten-hour day at my corporate job. Collect the truck, return home and restock. Home at 8.00pm.
- Thursday – truck open along the river. Ten-hour day at my corporate job. Collect the truck, return home and restock. Drive the truck to Hampton Court Palace for *Concours of Elegance* event set up. Home at 10.00pm.
- Friday - Day one at *Concours of Elegance*. Three coffee activations (coffee truck plus two private coffee enclosures). 3,000 people expected to attend today. Home at 10.00pm.
- Saturday - Day two at *Concours of Elegance*. 5,500 people expected to attend. Home at 10.00pm.
- Sunday - Day three at *Concours of Elegance*. 4,000 people attending. Home at 9.00pm.
- Monday – 8.00am fly from London to Sydney for corporate work.
- Seven days later – fly from Sydney to Singapore for corporate work.
- Four days later – fly from Singapore to London. Open the truck two hours after landing at Heathrow Airport.

I had this schedule pinned to our fridge at home, and I'd stare at it as motivation in the same way a fighter hangs a picture of their opponent in the corner of their bathroom mirror before a fight.

Over three incredible days we scaled Dear Coco to include six baristas across three coffee activations, surrounded by 12,500 of Europe's high society and the world's rarest cars. But by the end of the week the extreme pace started to take its toll.

It was late Saturday night and I was in the kitchen talking to Emma, Coco was also there as she stayed up late to see her dad given we hadn't seen much of each other since last Sunday. I had just finished day six of seven of my Super Bowl Week. This week entailed one hundred and ten hours of corporate work, plus Dear Coco street trading, plus 3 x 3 day event activations at one of the world's most prestigious events. The human mind should not work these amounts of hours in one week, it's simply not healthy.

I was sitting in the kitchen listening to Emma talk to me about her day, and in slow motion I felt myself slipping away from reality. My mind literally fell off a cliff and I went completely vacant, like my soul had just left my body. I didn't realise it was happening until Emma got extremely worried about me – she looked deep into my cloudy eyes wondering where I'd gone. She sounded my name like she was trying to wake me up from a deep sleep. Coco was asking what was happening to dad and got upset at seeing me in body but not in mind or spirit. Emma ushered me to bed and kept an eye on me. Thank goodness I was at home when this happened and not driving the coffee truck home – I don't remember what happened.

It was painfully clear I'd hit burnout point. I was mentally and physically exhausted to the point my mind overheated and simply switched off. It's never happened to me before and it was a terrible, frightening situation I created by overworking my mind and body to deliver on promises I'd made. If you've seen movies where the character sinks beneath the water level and looks back up at their loved ones as they sink deeper and deeper, my experience in the kitchen felt very similar to that. I could hear Emma fading away as I slipped deeper beneath the surface. The rest is a blur.

Heading into my Super Bowl Week I was nervous about how it would make me feel. I've never shied away from hard work, but this week had me spooked. So many people were relying on me to deliver at scale, and with an exceedingly high degree of quality. In partnership with my corporate and small business teams I feel like we did exactly that. The work delivered that week was exceptional, on both sides of my shop. But the price of being the leader out front was one I had to pay, and pay in silence.

Leadership takes invisible effort, often performed in the dark away from the spotlight. But when the lights come on all anyone should see is graceful strength. Everyone who relied on me that week got exactly that, but what they didn't see was the mental and physical damage happening inside. Sometimes that's the price a leader must pay to deliver on their promises.

In five-days, my and my team's efforts generated £13,378 worth of revenue for Dear Coco, the equivalent of four weeks street trading. This put £6,300 directly into the hands of my young family to make our lives better. Was it worth it? Yes, it's my job as leader, father and husband to make it worth it. But it left a scar, a kind of high tide mark in my mind that I now use to determine what rhythm is reasonable versus what should be approached with extreme caution, or avoided altogether.

The Flat White Economy

Having our two teenage daughters work as barista assistants on weekends is incredibly valuable to not only the business, but to them as young people.

Working alongside a 'full-sized' barista for five-hours on a weekend they get to see the value of money in real-time, and they see the importance of being punctual. Standing side-by-side with market leading-baristas they get to see what professionalism looks like; they experience how to endure tough conditions with an unrelenting dedication to work ethic and customer experience; they see what dad's efforts leading up to and after service contribute to the operations of the business. They see how hard it is to make money.

Before Dear Coco our girls only ever knew my corporate salary dropped into our bank account every month. I'm not in a sales or commission-based role so the amount of money is the same no matter what kind of month I had or how hard I worked. They couldn't connect that amount of money to the effort expelled to earn it, it just appeared. And that's entirely my job - to protect our kids from needing to worry about money at such a young age. They need to feel protected, they need to know Emma and I have everything under control.

Dear Coco shows the girls what it takes to make £10, £100, £1,000. When they say they'd like or need something, they can now connect it back to how many flat whites had to go over the counter to make it possible. That said, I'm careful not to create any guilt when Emma and I need to buy them things, they shouldn't feel any guilt for our responsibilities as parents. But it's entirely healthy for them to be able to equate new shoes with the effort required to buy them – mine and theirs. As a result of Dear Coco and their roles within it, they cherish the possessions they have and understand the value of money.

The power of part-time jobs for teenagers is immense, and giving our girls paid employment is not charity by any means, Dear Coco deeply relies on them on weekends to support our lead barista to deliver £800-£1,000 a day in sales. It's a one-and-a-half person job on weekends, that's for sure. Working behind a small, single group espresso machine isn't enough equipment for two full-sized baristas to operate efficiently. Having one lead barista loading and unloading the portafilter, steaming milk and pouring drinks, while an assistant puts transactions through the till, grinds and tamps fresh coffee and serves the retail products is the ideal staffing mix.

As I'm typing this book chapter at my dining table, our lead barista and Malia have just set a new daily sales record for the business. Prior to today our record was £1,006, but the team have just passed £1,070 with thirty minutes remaining on the clock. This is an amazing accomplishment and I'm deeply proud of the team and our customers for making it happen. But what's more pleasing about this is our family WhatsApp group has been alive with pride all afternoon. All of us (sorry Coco, you'll have your own phone someday) have been cheering on Malia and the business as this special day unfolds. The togetherness this tiny coffee truck has created is one of its most precious superpowers, and I know once the girls have graduated to full-time jobs they will look back on their time along the river as formative and fun.

As I designed and built Dear Coco in early 2021, the girls would openly dream about how amazing it was going to be to have a 'real job', earn money and be part of something special. In April 2021 as our new branded stickers, blank cups, plain white pastry bags and all the disposables arrived in the lead up to opening in May, it was a debate about who got to put the first sticker on the first cup. The kids would scramble to fill the little sweets bags to the exact 150g weight. Everyone wanted to stamp the Dear Coco logo in the bottom right corner of the pastry bags with the perfect one-centimetre border to the right and below. What a beautiful, meaningful project it was for our family right from the start, and it's continued to this day.

When the reality of launching the business and standing on the street came to bear, the girls were nervous but they knew they could take shelter behind me and not feel too exposed too soon. Once the business was paid off and it was time to expand the team, it put our teenage girls out of their comfort zone. This was the first time they had to work alongside someone other than me for an extended period and make conversation on their own. This was of equal if not more value to me than giving them exposure to the business from a financial standpoint. This taught them how to conduct themselves socially with adults who were not their parents and turn up to work on time because it's not dad relying on them, it's a professional barista. Emma and I have been so deeply grateful that our entire barista team have treated Malia and Lani like little sisters. They adore spending time with them and treat them with care and respect.

We have a hard and fast rule for the girls when working shifts at Dear Coco – the truck is a technology-free zone. They're instructed to leave their phones in the front cabin for the duration of their shift. When it's quiet they make conversation with their co-worker, clean down their area, re-stock the bakes and so on. I won't dive down the rabbit hole of young people's relationships with their digital devices, it's the world they were born into so adults can't begrudge them for it. But for a guy born in 1978 who's lived an analogue life before learning a newer digital world, I'm uniquely positioned to see value in force-feeding some analogue time into their digital lives. The truck puts them in a sort of digital purgatory for a few short hours a week, and I adore that.

As Malia and Lani inevitably turn their minds to other part-time jobs when they conclude their studies, I find myself encouraging them to pursue work in the coffee industry. No doubt once they graduate high school or university they'll want to leave London and explore the world. Travelling as a qualified barista would put them at the epicentre of culture wherever they go. According to the National Coffee Association, coffee is the world's most consumed beverage aside from water – it's an important part of societal norms. Culture is inherently infused in coffee, and cafés help create cultural experiences. Put simply, coffee is a connector of people no matter their race, religion, creed or beliefs. Coffee would be a beautiful art form for them to master before they set sail on their adventures far and wide.

~~~~

All businesses experience staff attrition, it's all part of being in business. But little did I expect our first resignation to come from so deep within our little organisation. Coco, the seven-year-old namesake of the business, shocked the Dear Coco Limited Executive Team (Emma and I) to the core back in July 2023.

Since we launched the business in 2021 Coco has been desperate to help however humanly possible, she just wanted to be involved. Recognising her enthusiasm, Emma and I took a chance on this unknown, unproven rookie. We assigned her the pivotal role of Chief Counter Sign Maker, effective immediately with no probation period. The salary wasn't competitive given all the negotiating power sat with Emma and me, but we were quietly confident the remuneration package was more than generous. This included lifelong love, a place to live, endless food and drink, access to a wide variety of teddies, two older sisters, and a life full of school pickups, play dates, and cinema visits. We shook on the deal and welcomed Coco as our first ever Chief Counter Sign Maker.

Coco's daily responsibilities were simple – I'd read out the bake names to be served at the truck the following day. In her neatest writing Coco would write down what I was saying, sometimes asking me to spell the words in child lettering. She'd then search through the pile of loose magnetic letters and stick them to the metal counter signs, along with the associated prices. She'd then use the long edge of an empty counter sign to make the letters nice and straight. I know I know, it's a big job that might intimidate many seven-year-olds, but not our Coco – she's a rockstar.

From day one Coco immersed herself in her new 'C-Suite role'. She showed on up time (always after dinner); went to the correct location (the dining room table); was always dressed for work (in pyjamas); came prepared with the right tools (paper and felt tip pens, in all colours); and brought a crew to ensure adequate support (her Big Bear teddy). Day after day, Coco performed her duties to role-model standard and she was on track to receive a glowing mid-year review. Emma and I were beyond happy with her performance; it was like she'd been doing the role her whole life. It was everything we could do to make Coco feel rewarded and recognised. Talent like this comes along once in a generation, so we needed to make it impossible for her to leave or be tempted away by a better (unpaid) offer!

Then, one balmy summer evening it all fell apart. I walked into the dining room to check on Coco and something just felt off. I couldn't put my finger on it, but I could sense some unrest in the air. You know when you walk into a room and two people have just had an argument – the tension is palpable. A similar feeling of unrest was quietly reverberating around the dining room as Coco sat at the table performing her duties. I ignored any natural intuition I had and went back into the kitchen to finish cooking dinner. I was gone maybe ten minutes and things were awfully quiet in the dining room. Normally there's the constant flow of chatter and questions coming from Coco around all matters work and life, but at this moment things were eerily quiet. With my chef's towel and wooden spatula still in hand I went to check on Coco, only to discover something that rocked me to my core.

Lying on the dining table under a mess of loose magnetic letters and blank metal counter signs was a handwritten note. Written in cold, grey pencil was a note I'll never forget. If Dear Coco Limited was a publicly listed company, in this moment our share price would've spiralled into freefall. This note (correction, this dagger to the heart) contained words so indifferent and emotionless I wondered whether Coco was ever happy in her role of Chief Counter Sign Maker at Dear Coco Limited:

"Dad I do not want to anymore. From Coco"

Curt, heartless, thankless, self-centred. These are the words that came to mind as I read Coco's resignation note from the role we created for her only weeks earlier. I felt hurt, used and let down. I knew we'd never find anyone quite like Coco to perform this role going forward, so I went into damage control. I went upstairs to her room and begged her to reconsider. She wouldn't even talk about it. I told her I'd throw in a brownie if she reconsidered – I had 30 freshly baked portions downstairs that were awaiting their counter sign (ironic). She didn't accept the offer. Coco was all business and the look on her face was clear, she wanted out and she didn't want to talk about it. There was nothing I could do, so I demonstrated courageous leadership and simply shook hands, wished her well and left her room.

Nothing stops the Dear Coco machine, not even disruption like this at the executive level. That night I did what all good leaders do, I rolled up my sleeves, finished the counter signs including the particularly emotional sign for *Raspberry and Coconut Brownie (vegan, gf) £2.80* – the bake used as my last attempt to tempt Coco into reconsidering. Maybe the length of this sign and sheer volume of letters required was the straw that broke Coco's back? Who knows, but in an act of emotional protection I haven't ordered this bake since!

I lost something that night, I lost faith in small people. Now if you ever need me after dinnertime and before my corporate calls with Australia and New York commence, you'll find me at our dining room table making counter signs for the following day. I haven't been able to replace Coco since her resignation, nor could I ever envisage anyone else in this pivotal role – she made it her own. We wish you well in your future endeavours, Coco. Thank you for all you did for Dear Coco Limited, references are available on request.

Top 5

In July 2022 I was being driven around the bumpy cobblestone streets of Lisbon, Portugal feeling incredibly car sick. I was in Lisbon for two days attending a series of meetings for my corporate job, and the entire trip was spent snaking our way around central Lisbon attending meeting after meeting. It was the middle of summer and it was devilishly hot. To make it worse every taxi driver seemed to refuse to turn on their air conditioning given they were used to the heat and/or didn't want the associated impact on their car's petrol consumption. Every car we got into was roasting hot, and being dressed in full business attire certainly didn't help. As a result I was feeling car sick from the heat and bumpy, hilly streets of Lisbon where we spent hour after hour being chauffeured around.

We all know the last thing you should do when feeling car sick is read or check your phone, it's the fastest way to feeling even worse. But given the amount of time we were spending in cars and meetings I needed to keep some work things moving back in London via email, so I had to brave the inevitable and use my phone in the car.

Stopped at a set of traffic lights, I took a quick break from emails and flicked over to Instagram to give my mind a quick rest by watching some Reels. Away from curating the Dear Coco Instagram feed and watching surf videos online, I'm not a heavy user of social media. The content served up to me by the algorithm is mostly coffee related, surfing clips, fail videos, and pug dogs riding skateboards because I stupidly hovered over a similar video a week ago, and now wish I hadn't.

Sitting at the traffic lights I opened Instagram and what immediately caught my eye was the love heart icon in the top right hand corner of the screen – this icon shows the volume of new followers, mentions and likes Dear Coco has received since I last opened the app. This number was ginormous and I had no idea why. It had been a day or so since my last post, and even my most impressive content wouldn't drive the level of new engagement I was seeing. I eventually figured it out, someone had tagged Dear Coco in a post and that was driving a whole new audience to our feed. I navigated to the post and associated online magazine article where Dear Coco was featured, and my heart filled with joy seeing Dear Coco had just been featured in *Barista Magazine* as a leading coffee truck of the world. It stood to reason my car sickness immediately vanished and the car heat became a complete non-issue. I couldn't read the article fast enough, partly due to my excitement, but mostly because the taxi was now moving again and the danger of vomiting was once again very real.

The online article was written by a well-respected industry writer for *Barista Magazine* who had scoured the world of coffee trucks and listed five businesses as the ones doing a standout job. The list included trucks from Sweden, France, Romania, Japan and Dear Coco in London. Some of these trucks I knew from my general awareness of the street coffee category, while some were completely new to me. I took immense interest and pride in seeing these magnificent little businesses from all corners of the world sitting next to Dear Coco being labelled the best by an industry-leading publication. As comments of 'thanks' and 'honoured' came from the fellow truck owners in response to their own inclusion, an instant comradery was formed on social media between us owners. What a beautiful, honourable group to be a part of.

When I got back to the hotel later that night and had time to digest the full article, my mind turned to how I would fold this industry recognition into the Dear Coco story. The marketer within me knew the potential power of this recognition, while the more modest father-of-three talked it down as not a formal award judged by a panel of industry leaders. This was an industry author doing a global coffee truck search from her home in the US, making all kinds of assumptions about what was good and wasn't good about these businesses. She didn't visit Dear Coco or any other truck on the Top 5 list to assess us against set criteria or rank us accordingly. This list of coffee trucks was a matter of one person's opinion, albeit a respected and credible one.

My marketing and rational brains collided, and I thought about what it's actually acknowledging. I reflected on the progress Dear Coco had made since launching fourteen months earlier. I thought about our utter dedication to quality and the commitment of everyone involved in the business, including the producers of the world-class products we sell. I thought about how our business delivers excellence in extremely challenging conditions in unarguably the toughest category in coffee. So in this moment I decided to stand proud as founder of a business that by anyone's measure would be labelled world-class. From that moment on our business would be referred to as:

Dear Coco, Top 5 Global Coffee Truck as featured in Barista Magazine

I wrestled with the lack of criteria the top 5 trucks were measured against, and that this author didn't visit any of these businesses to benchmark the industry against us. But in the absence of any street coffee recognition programme or opportunities to submit Dear Coco for a category award, I figured this list was as good as anything.

Once the comfort of naming Dear Coco a Top 5 Global Coffee Truck settled, it got me thinking about what we'd achieved since that December 2020 evening when I stood in the kitchen and asked Emma to support my invisible dream. Even though I came with hospitality experience to help inform some sort of business operation, I had zero experience in coffee trucks or building a brand from scratch. In 2020 I asked Emma to trust me with our life savings during an incredibly unstable time financially and emotionally, and I assured her I could do a good job. One-and-a-half years later I was now sitting in a hotel room in Lisbon as Founder of *Dear Coco, Top 5 Global Coffee Truck as featured in Barista Magazine.*

This made me immensely proud of the team and everyone who contributes to our success, but if I'm totally honest I'm most proud of Emma and me. We're the ones who showed courage and commitment to risk everything we had on a dream. We're the ones who grind it out day after day to put the truck on the street while maintaining a perfectly balanced, happy family life. Going one egotistic, selfish step further I'm immensely proud of myself as the guy who puts himself on a ledge day after day with vulnerable, transparent storytelling that captured the attention of the coffee world. *Barista Magazine* most certainly would never have found Dear Coco along the River Thames in London if our digital presence wasn't as powerful as it is, and didn't fit the phenomenal in-person experience we've created. I'm completely at peace with marketing Dear Coco's lofty position within the global coffee industry, and I'm immensely proud of it whether we have a physical trophy to validate our status or not.

Chapter 9
Decision #3. Expansion

For two years our success with the coffee truck was hard-earned. We outperformed every target we set ourselves, our revenue grew year-on-year, we became famous in the local area and respected amongst the global coffee community, and we helped elevate the London street coffee scene. It's one of those beautiful success stories to emerge from the devastation of a global pandemic. More importantly, the business has given me the creative outlet I so desperately needed and it's allowed me to financially provide for the family within the quiet safety of West London.

Knowing this, why would a guy who has everything he fought hard to achieve risk it all (again) to expand into a brick-and-mortar cafe? Greed? Ego? Maybe both. Why after working so damn hard for six years to financially rebuild after relocating from Sydney to London? Why after losing our life savings solving significant UK visa and settlement complications? Why after taking a backward step in my corporate career and having to bartend secretly at night to pay our over-inflated Chiswick bills? Why after risking our rebuilt life savings to build a coffee truck dream that existed only in my head? Why after working seven days a week for five straight months to launch the coffee truck, nearly breaking myself in the process? These were the questions I asked myself on repeat as I tossed and turned every night early in 2023.

For coffee truck owners expansion into physical cafés is a well-trodden path, I wonder why though. Do we view the street as a mere entry point for the 'main game' of brick-

and-mortar? Are truck tyres sitting on the bitumen deemed not deep enough roots to embed ourselves within the community? Perhaps the allure of a front door and walls to keep the cold (and the occasional dickhead) out is just too damn appealing! The reality of street coffee is harsh, so it stands to reason that coffee truck owners want to evolve.

Up until that moment I never had the inclination to add to the Dear Coco portfolio with a physical café space. With years of hospitality experience in my back pocket I felt like I knew too much, if that's even a thing. I knew how thin net profit margins are; I knew that one fixed cost as simple as rent can be powerful enough to make or break a business. I knew I'd spend 60% of my time worrying about something that occupies 30% of my balance sheet – the critical shortage of London specialty coffee baristas and the headaches this creates. I knew that six to twelve months of below-forecast trade would likely result in the business closing before the lease break-clause had been reached and the initial fit-out investment had been recouped. I knew the immense pressure and stress that comes with owning a café, I'd worked for venue owners for years and saw the impact it had on their personal lives. Taking an eight-to-fifteen-year lease on a fixed café space is not for the faint hearted.

~~~~

It was February 2023 and the coffee truck was winning. For two years we'd seen unstoppable, consistent growth. Our Instagram presence passed 10,000 followers (an obscene number for such a tiny coffee truck with one location in under two years). We had the best barista team and supplier network, and we're a well-managed business making 35-40% net profit. Life tasted like gravy. Each night I'd sit back in my chair listening to the happy chatter around the family dinner table and feel immense gratitude that the life we'd created finally felt stable and light. I had everything I needed and more.

Then, BOOM! Fifteen minutes down the road from Dear Coco my favourite specialty coffee shop announced its permanent closure. Within days the café staff were laid off, newspaper was taped to the windows and the equipment got stripped out. Finito. The owner just didn't have it in her anymore. It happens. Running a coffee business, or any business for that matter, is a grind (pun intended and achieved). I was sad to see an owner who likely worked as hard as me lose their dream, I was sad to see a team of baristas lose their jobs without much warning, and I was sad as a customer that adored this beautiful little coffee shop.

But amongst this admittedly surface-level sadness my opportunistic brain kicked into overdrive. When I got home that night Emma and I stayed at the kitchen table after the kids adjourned. I brought Emma up to speed with the café news I'd received earlier that day and the opportunistic thoughts running through my mind ever since. We spoke about whether this should even mean anything to us given we already had everything we set out to achieve. We also spoke about what we wanted our individual and combined futures to look like from a professional perspective.

Emma is an immensely talented person who finds her own motivation and drive working alone at home. Although she loves her business and clients, being self-employed can be a lonely life. As a result, Emma was open to exploring alternative careers to bring her closer to her Chiswick community. As for me, I adore the challenge of being a Marketing Director within a large multinational organisation. It puts me at the table alongside the world's best marketers and strategic thinkers where I learn an immeasurable amount. Yet at some point both Emma and I envisage coffee playing a more dominant role in our professional lives. For Emma, it was to connect with her community in a new meaningful way, and for me it was to take everything I learned in big business and be a coffee entrepreneur full-time. We spoke about using this vacant shop as the natural next step to scale Dear Coco beyond the truck and create opportunities for us both to live the professional lives we were starting to crave.

For the third time in eight years Emma and I made a monumental life decision: we were getting into the brick-and-mortar café business. This decision was made despite the fact I already knew all the challenges and likely scenarios that lay ahead. We led with our hearts while we convinced our heads we were commercially astute enough to make this business work long-term, flying in the face of the statistical likelihood we wouldn't succeed past our first two to four years.

The following day I picked up the phone to some local coffee contacts asking for the landlady's phone number. She'd just lost her tenant of four years when she was expecting them to stay for eight. I want to speak to her; I want to get to her before the property hits the real estate market and *Blank Street* likely gobble it up with their aggressive UK expansion. The café site is around the corner from our house, it's a corner block with good passing foot traffic overlooking a beautifully manicured park. In short, it's a great spot for specialty coffee and bakes.

I tracked down the landlady and invited her to chat about her now empty shop, and we agreed to meet in a café around the corner from her property. I strategically invited Emma and Coco – who picked out her prettiest dress for the occasion – as I wanted to create emotional impact.

Days later we met the landlady with a warm introduction outside her empty premises, before adjourning to the café around the corner. I told her our origin story (smile on cue please, Coco), I told her the story of our ambition to expand into brick-and-mortar and that this site was the only one we wanted. The landlady was particularly attached to her shop, so winning her heart *and* her commercial mind was key. I told her I was connected to her shop after being a customer for four years, and how some of my happiest moments were spent in the little front window playing *Memory* with Coco on the table slightly too small to rest all the cards.

The sales pitch came out seamlessly and Coco's pretty dress worked a treat. We verbally agreed terms for a new eight year lease, shook hands and fetched the solicitors to make it happen. I hired a shiny big city solicitor; the landlady hired a less-shiny suburban one, and away they went about commencing the lease negotiation and contract process.

Within days cracks started to appear. Our side moved decisively; their side didn't. Our side practiced proper commercial law; their side didn't. Our side worked to balance risk where risk was unavoidable; their side – you guessed it – didn't. To make things more complicated, given the outgoing tenant was forfeiting her lease early and allowing her fourth year break-clause to pass, she needed to contribute to the process to surrender the lease so a new one could be issued. This added a third solicitor into the mix, and three is rarely better than two.

According to our solicitor, to agree a standard commercial lease at this simple level should take about six weeks. We pushed forward and secured a builder; we lined up suppliers; we designed the interiors and we hired staff. We planned everything down to the last detail while avoiding investing too much money until the lease was signed. We negotiated a one-month rent-free period to complete a light renovation of the space before we opened, which would take the entire rent-free period. We moved diligently at speed so once we signed the lease we'd hit go on everything to maximise the rent-free period and open as soon as possible. Overnight £50,000 would leave our family savings account in pursuit of this new dream of having a front door and walls that kept the cold out.

It was now official – I was putting the family in financial harm's way (again) after rebuilding following our move to London, then launching a street coffee business. *What the heck am I doing?* I'd ask myself. I didn't even have plans to expand into a brick-and-mortar café a few weeks ago, now it's become the biggest single thing in our life. There was an undercurrent of intense nervousness as I put my head on the pillow each night, but it was the same when building the coffee truck, so I'd write it off as completely natural.

Things were moving forward, but not at the pace I expected on the legal side. And then, BOOM, the outgoing tenant vanished off the face of the earth. She literally disappeared and no one knew where she'd gone. This was a major problem given we couldn't progress the lease process without her - we needed her paperwork, certificates, foreclosures and ultimately her signature. Why would someone completely renege on their responsibilities of concluding a process that they'd created by walking out on their café mid-lease? Surely she couldn't bury her head in the sand on this one? She was still paying rent on her empty café until the new incoming tenant (Dear Coco) signed the new lease, in turn releasing her from all ongoing responsibilities.

The outgoing tenant's lawyer was eventually able to track down his client and have a brief conversation. It turned out this rich kid of an industry tycoon deemed the foreclosure of her lease, and the responsibilities that came with it, an inconvenience. Under the cloak of darkness she walked away only to be found (via a quick Instagram search) in Southern Europe burying her proverbial head in a bucket of chilled rosé. All three lawyers continued their efforts to make contact with the tenant, but frustratingly she ignored everyone and turned her back on all her responsibilities. Things got so desperate that I sent her a text message essentially begging her to complete her outstanding tasks so we could move into the property. I told her about the two staff members who were in limbo without work while she dragged out the process, and that we had teams of people waiting in a holding pattern to start work on the project. Sadly she never replied, and the delays continued.

The contract process expected to take six weeks turned into nineteen excruciating weeks. The barista team I hired to commence thirteen weeks earlier needed serious financial support, we all thought they'd be enjoying paid employment in the Dear Coco Coffee Shop by now. Even though we hadn't exchanged employment contracts with the team I felt entirely responsible for them. They'd bought into the Dear Coco dream I sold them and they continued to stay committed amongst the uncertainty.

The only tool in my arsenal was the coffee truck, currently only operating Wednesdays to Sundays along the river. I decided to open the business on Mondays and Tuesdays each week to create more shifts and keep the team going financially. I wasn't licenced to trade along the river on Mondays and Tuesdays at the time so, similar to when we relocated the business to Hammersmith many months earlier, I knocked on doors searching for private land to trade on. I found a large residential development recently completed not far from Strand on the Green that said they'd be delighted to have us on their land Mondays and Tuesdays for as long as we needed, and they wouldn't even charge me a daily pitch fee (the coffee truck equivalent of rent). Along with Jon and the Manager of Linden House, Dear Coco now had a third saviour.

To make this arrangement work all we needed to do was to make £220 a day in sales to break-even. At £220 I could pay the barista wages and daily operating costs, but the profit would be zero for all the extra work I needed to perform to open and close the business. Essentially I'd be working for free to pay people, yet this felt like a win so long as the team could financially survive. After weeks of trading at our temporary location we barely achieved our £220 daily sales target. I made no money for the family despite all this additional work, and burnout threatened me once again. But the priority was paying our baristas while Little Miss Rich Kid chilled more European rosé (sorry I'm still bitter).

This intense period of time resulted in me working seventy-five days straight without a single day off. I told myself this commercial real estate thing is a mug's game. Sitting at my kitchen table watching my family giggling away was now a thing of the past. *What have I done?* I knew that I knew too much about this stupid hospitality game, yet I ignored my own intuition. I led with my heart and now look where it took me.

~~~~

Nineteen weeks into the lease process and I was having a quiet coffee in Chiswick with the sun on my face. I was absolutely exhausted from working seven days a week with the world sitting on my shoulders. My phone rang. It was an industry friend I trusted.

"Ant, I've just heard there's a new specialty coffee shop opening directly across the road from your new shop. They've moved fast and it's opening in four weeks".

On hearing the news I told myself competition is good, competition is inevitable, but something felt off. As I sipped my coffee I opened Google Maps and took a screenshot of the local area. I circled in green the existing (credible) coffee shops and in red I circled the three new coffee shops that had opened since I started the lease process in February. One new competitor was directly around the corner from "our" shop; one competitor intercepted a major pedestrian flow from Chiswick High Road; the other intercepted foot traffic from Bedford Park. Our shop was now flanked by new and established coffee shops to the point it made the area feel over-saturated.

In the nineteen weeks we'd spent on the lease negotiations the competitive landscape around Turnham Green had altered. My assessment was the area simply did not need, and couldn't support, another specialty coffee shop, no matter how good we knew we could be. But pure gut feeling wasn't enough to sabotage this 'dream', so I strapped on my propeller hat and crunched some numbers. My assessment was these three new competitors with their intercepting positions would reduce Dear Coco's shop revenue by 15-20%. I was forecasting our new shop to generate £6,000 per week in sales with a net profit of approximately 15%. As owners the only money we'd make from this shop is the net profit, so I was fiercely protective of this number.

You don't need an economics degree to realise that if our revenue goes down by 15-20%, our expected net profit of 15% was no longer workable. Not only would we be working for free, but our £50,000 initial investment couldn't be replenished. Any unexpected dip in sales, maintenance issues or Act of God would cause real issues and I'd then be relying on profits generated from the coffee truck to prop up the shop. At that point the gravy turns to turpentine.

I finished my coffee and walked home. Emma was at her desk in the living room and I asked if we could have a chat in the kitchen – most big conversations seem to happen in our kitchen. I gave her the update on the conversation I just had with my industry friend and the subsequent competitor research I'd done. We needed to have a chat about where to go from here. We spoke about all the work we'd put into the new shop up until this moment and what a shame it would be to walk away. We spoke about why we were even entertaining the notion of opening a café to begin with. We spoke about the journey we'd been on for the past five years and the feeling of contentment we were now blessed to have after so many years of struggle. We spoke about fate, and that perhaps if something needed to be pushed so hard then it's not meant to happen.

Anyone who knows Emma will agree she's the most incredible, supportive person. She knows when to be decisive and when to let the process take its course. She asked me what I wanted to do about the shop, knowing I'd talk myself into a resolution that would make sense for all of us. I'm an incredibly decisive person, so this decision wouldn't sit with me for long.

Not one to shy away from expressing emotion, in this pivotal moment I broke down in tears in front of Emma. I recounted tales of the immense pressure I felt personally over the past fifteen years. The role of primary financial provider for a family of five is intense, sometimes suffocating. My reality as financial leader of the family is I can never stop; I can never walk away to catch my breath; I can never say it's all too hard. Like most people I simply have to keep going, no matter the circumstances or state of mind.

The forcefield of confidence in my mind that once surrounded the Dear Coco Coffee Shop had now been compromised, and I no longer felt we could win the hospitality war. It felt like the odds were stacked against us and the stress-free contentment we'd worked so hard to achieve was now at risk. And for what, a dream that didn't even exist until the tenant at my favourite coffee shop decided to walk out on her business? That's not a dream, that's an opportunity, and they're very different things. I cried while hugging Emma, saying I couldn't go back to that time when I couldn't sleep because I was so worried about money. I told her we can walk away from this opportunity as easily as it landed in our laps – we've got too much to lose and rebuild if we fail. I didn't have another rebuild in me after our move to London, the Dear Coco coffee truck, and the always-on demands of a corporate job.

So that was it – we were out! We made the agonising decision not to complete the lease we'd spent the last nineteen weeks begging for. The following day was like cancelling a wedding the week before the bride and groom were due to walk down the aisle. I called our two gorgeous coffee shop staff members to break the news; this made me cry. I informed the three solicitors; this did not make me cry. I informed our kids, our coffee roastery, our builder, electrician, suppliers, ceramics lady, awning crew and our designer. They were all devastated for us as they knew how much work had gone into moulding this opportunity into a dream.

It was the right commercial decision, but damn it was hard. I was emotionally invested in the potential of a front door and walls that kept the cold out. In a funny sliding doors moment, without Little Miss Rich Kid's vanishing act we would have signed the lease and found ourselves trapped in an unwinnable situation – so the rosé is on me if we bump into each other down the road.

But as the disappointment dissipated and our lovely shop team found new roles, it was time for reflection. Here's what I learned over these nineteen weeks going from street coffee truck to brick-and-mortar… and back again:

- Common sense isn't common.

- Be humble. You can't beat everyone.
- It ain't done until it's done. Invest accordingly.
- True character is shown in moments of chaos.
- If the deal isn't right, it's wrong. Be decisive.
- Don't let your heart dominate your head. Both have a role at different times.
- No one likes spoiled rich kids. But sometimes their indifference can play a role.
- It's not how big it is, it's what you do with it. Our tiny coffee truck makes our family more net profit than a brick-and-mortar café, with half the revenue.

Below are our 2022 Chiswick Coffee Truck financials versus our year one shop forecast, to help demonstrate the net profit scenario of truck versus brick-and-mortar café:

Dear Coco Chiswick Coffee Truck (2022 actuals in GBP) Trading 5 days per week		Dear Coco Coffee Shop (Year one forecast in GBP) Trading 7 days per week	
Total Revenue	£144,560	Total Revenue	£305,000
Rent	£1,100	Rent	£25,000
Business Rates	£0	Business Rates	£2,600
Wages	£27,500	Wages	£84,776
Utilities	£1,560	Utilities	£18,000
Coffee costs	£18,792	Coffee costs	£37,000
Bakes costs	£10,119	Bakes costs	£20,000
Milk costs	£4,336	Milk costs	£7,800
Disposables	£4,550	Disposables	£8,000

Miscellaneous costs	£1,331	Miscellaneous costs	£10,400
Value Added Tax	£17,347	Value Added Tax	£46,000
Net Profit (GBP)	**£57,925**	**Net Profit (GBP)**	**£45,424**
Net Profit (%)	**40%**	**Net Profit (%)**	**14.9%**

Some tough life and business lessons were learned on this one, and a tonne of precious family savings vanished into the abyss with no tangible result. Although we tried hard to minimise investments until the lease was signed, we lost £6,000 to the project in legal fees and other pre-ordered elements due to lengthy production timeframes.

There's a saying in commercial real estate that "time kills deals!" It now appears so does Southern European rosé.

~~~~

At the time of writing, the café that many months later agreed the lease and moved into that beautiful corner block has struggled to find traction. At key service moments in the mornings and afternoons, as well as on weekends, the café is not attracting the foot traffic required to make the site sustainable and successful. Of course we wish them the utmost luck in finding success, however it feels like the guy who felt he knew too much about the hospitality industry might be proven correct.

Chapter 10
To the Moon

On a Sunday morning in December 2023 my Instagram and LinkedIn accounts lit up with two messages that made me realise just how powerful Dear Coco and my approach to ownership had become. The messages were uniquely crafted for each platform, which told me the author had taken time and effort.

Around that time Dear Coco passed 17,000 followers on Instagram and 4,000 people followed me on LinkedIn. A by-product of these burgeoning followerships meant there were no shortages of people wanting to 'talk business', 'invest in Dear Coco's future' or 'scale us globally'. A seemingly endless supply of advisors and investors wanted to get a piece of Dear Coco and scale what I've deliberately kept rare until this point. I'm honoured that so many people make contact with me, but I've always insisted that I'll run this race at my own pace.

My typical approach to replying to business-related messages on social media is to show deliberate brevity. I need a turnkey way to filter out the fakers and bring the more serious investors to the surface, should they appear. So on this Sunday morning this well-rehearsed routine played out again, only this time it featured the same investor across two different platforms, with messages arriving within moments of each other. This outreach felt different to the others, but nevertheless I replied with my typically short, indifferent response. I thanked the author for their interest in Dear Coco and requested they send me a high-level overview of their thinking so I can assess any potential next steps. It's usually at this point most suitors vanish, which suits me perfectly, I only want to talk to potential business partners who have proactively invested some initial thinking into Dear Coco.

The response I received to my curt reply confirmed my suspicion that this outreach was indeed different to the others. I not only heard back from my suitor, but within an hour I received a detailed, thoughtful, articulate response that outlined who they were; why they contacted me; their investment appetite for Dear Coco; the impact on the coffee industry they wanted to make and so on. I was blown away by the considered nature of their response, one clearly crafted by a person with a superior level of commercial intelligence, small business EQ and respect for the journey I was already on with Dear Coco. Based on this considered, thoughtful response I told myself this was most certainly a person I was interested in speaking to. A series of very pleasant, constructive messages throughout the morning concluded with us agreeing on a face-to-face meeting when they were next due in London, around three weeks' time. We shook digital hands, agreed we'd be in contact within two weeks to finalise the meeting arrangements and went our separate ways, both buzzing from our brief encounter.

Before I got on with the rest of my day my natural curiosity kicked into overdrive, and I wanted to understand more about this person I'd just agreed to meet. I started a Google search on my phone to understand exactly who I was dealing with, and a thirty second cursory search revealed all I needed to know.

Sam Chandler is a former private and public company CEO; startup founder; serial entrepreneur; renowned business builder; father; Australian coffee tragic and now investor. Sam founded, took public and recently sold his software company, Nitro, to a private equity firm for over half a billion dollars.

OK, things had just got very, very interesting.

During our initial exchange Sam told me since he sold Nitro he established a family office to invest in people and businesses he finds inspiring, interesting and unique. I was honoured he was now lining up a meeting with little old me – Ant Duckworth, Founder of Dear Coco Coffee, the Aussie surfer, family man and dream chaser who's been on a rollercoaster ride for the past few years trying to put his life back together. I was beyond humbled and incredibly excited about what might happen in a few weeks' time, I felt like I was getting ready to appear on an episode of the small business investment show *Shark Tank*.

As the meeting drew closer I told Emma on more than one occasion there's a 99% chance this meeting will be a productive, energising conversation over lunch that likely won't progress any further. I did this partly to manage her expectations but also my own. I'm naturally a confident person, but where could this new investor relationship possibly go, really? It was a meeting between the guy who founded quite possibly the smallest coffee business by square meterage on the planet, and a person who created and sold their Silicon Valley technology company for over half a billion dollars. A greater mismatch had never existed, so I was cautious to think any further ahead other than what plate of food I'd enjoy at our lunch meeting and how much I could learn from spending an hour or so with a very talented business person.

As the date of the meeting approached I talked to myself while lying awake in bed at night, asking myself things like *What if this meeting between two talented, passionate professionals is actually the 1% moment that changes my life?* That's how it happens for some people, right? So why not me, why not *this* meeting?

The day arrived when Sam travelled to meet me in Chiswick. We of course arranged to meet for coffee at Dear Coco before adjourning to a private meeting room in a pub further along the river. I don't typically get nervous before business meetings and that day was no different, I was completely relaxed and excited to meet a new friend. Sam arrived at the truck and our connection felt relaxed right from the start. We enjoyed a coffee standing by the river; we made conversation with a few regular customers of Dear Coco; we then headed to the pub. It was only a five minute walk, so it was nice to chat casually before we entered the pub and put our business hats on.

Inside it was quiet, almost empty, so we decided not to utilise the private meeting room. Instead we sat in the restaurant and ordered some water and a bottle of wine to toast our new connection. My style when meeting a new business acquaintance for the first time is to prolong the small talk period as long as humanly possible before we start talking business. I'm all about building early rapport, so spending what might feel like an inordinate amount of time talking about family, our backgrounds, likes, dislikes, travel, surfing, motorcycles or any manner of topics is how I like to create a sense of ease. Once you leave the rapport-building phase of the conversation and leap into business it's almost impossible to go back. In keeping with that approach, I asked personal question after question to keep the conversation down the warm end of the pool for as long as possible before we jumped into the deeper, colder business end.

Perhaps an hour had gone by and we hadn't yet uttered a single business word, and I felt like we knew each other at a much deeper level than our short history would normally allow. Knowing we'd built a solid bedrock it was at that point I felt comfortable to evolve the conversation into business. Although the purpose of the meeting might have created the same level of seriousness as an episode of *Shark Tank*, the reality on the day was a relaxed, highly energising conversation between two passionate, creative people.

What I expected to be a one hour meeting turned into a six and a half hour working session. Usually the energy within a conversation that length would start to decline over time, but not this one – the energy was on the ascendency the entire time and we expressed our disappointment when the time came to wrap things up.

During the session we spoke about my hopes and dreams for Dear Coco, and how these might align with what Sam was hoping to achieve with his next venture. We spoke about all sorts of opportunities ranging from franchising the coffee truck model, expansion into stand-alone brick-and-mortar cafés, coffee equipment automation, coffee roasteries, the works. We even spoke about the possibility of reactivating (at scale) my first-ever business venture that I built when I was twenty-five years old – an undercover restaurant and bar reviewing business called London Dry Venue Reviews. The energy around all the ideas discussed was palpable, but the inevitable end of the evening was fast approaching. As Sam ordered his Uber to take him back to the hotel I told myself it was time to bring out the two aces I'd been quietly holding up my sleeve the entire evening. I mean how often do you get to sit at the table with someone looking for ways to invest hundreds of thousands of pounds in you? I couldn't leave any cards up my sleeve. I was confident these two fresh ideas would take the conversation to a totally different level.

"Actually, I have two other ideas" I said out loud, and the room stood still. Sam's eyes fixated on me like I'd just produced the detailed location map of the Holy Grail. I said I had a combination of ideas that could make Dear Coco THE differentiated coffee company within a very traditional industry. A series of businesses circling around me, the relatable, nice guy of coffee.

I proposed we build a model of micro-footprint, low CapEx (Capital Expenditure), low OpEx (Operating Expenditure) businesses with uniquely high net profits and market positioning that we could scale quickly. The concept of 'small premium' suits the Dear Coco brand perfectly, and if these businesses can achieve high net profitability (like the Dear Coco Chiswick truck does) and can be scaled quickly then we'd have a highly valuable company. I also envisaged a series of other Dear Coco product-related businesses that we would build to fuel not only our own expansion plans, but other burgeoning parts of the coffee industry.

The second idea would focus more on me. I wanted to build a public profile forged off the back of what I've already become recognised for – the credible, nice guy of coffee that inspires and educates small business founders, parents and anyone who respects hard work, resilience and an iron will to succeed. There would be more books, maybe a film and television career, and of course product development and endorsements. This arm of the business would lovingly become known in that session as *Ant, Inc* (a temporary, working title). I figured the industry needed a positive, relatable person that coffee and non-coffee enthusiasts could relate to. *"Why not me?"* I asked out loud. I bring business acumen and credibility through my corporate career and small business endeavours; I have life experience; I've travelled the world extensively; I've made courageous decisions that put my family in harm's way and I emerged victorious.

Speaking out loud about these lofty ideas to such a highly credentialed business builder felt imposter-like, almost too confident to come from such a humble man's mouth. But the reaction these two ideas received pushed the last five hours' worth of other ideas completely off the table. I could see the idea wheel turning feverishly in Sam's mind, to the point where ordering the Uber became a distant memory and the conversation had reached an entirely new level. It was clear I'd hit the nail so squarely on the head that we could have stayed for dinner and spoken for another five hours on these two new ideas alone.

Sadly the evening had to conclude, many hours after we both expected it to. Sam and I shook hands and man-hugged and went our own ways feeling utterly energised by what had just happened. Whether it's an inspiring personal development course or a first date that went exceptionally well, it's natural for the energy to subside once you re-enter the real world. I didn't know what if any next steps might happen as the energy of this Ant x Sam moment subsided into the night, but I did know I gave it everything I had. I left no ideas on the table or passion in the tank. If Sam wanted to be part of Dear Coco I could have given no finer representation of our business or myself as founder. The rest was now out of my hands as I walked back to the truck to drive it home with a proud smile on my face.

As I lay in bed that night thinking about the brilliant day I had, I wanted to close things with a note of thanks to my new friend Sam for dedicating so much time to Dear Coco. As I lay my head on the pillow, mentally and emotionally drained, I sent the following message:

"What an energising meet...thank you. Tonight you asked me what I want, and I didn't fully answer. As the 70-year-old version of myself looking down the family table I want to feel certain things...undeniable, impactful, resourceful, happy. A guy who using humble tools owned the immense pressure of providing for a family while pursuing his dream of a maximised life.

Outside the family I want to leave a mark, which is already underway. 'Ant, Inc.' can impact lives at a business and personal level – a series of Dear Coco businesses circled around a published industry figurehead, each fuelling the other's success. At the centre is a guy so relatable and honest that with the right strategy and tools can generate commercial success, in real life and digitally.

I'm etching a future out of stone – I'd be honoured if you and your family came along for the ride. It'll be a fun journey however I get there. I'm on 07XXX XXX XXX if you want to step out onto the ledge and have a crack. Thank you for investing your day on a hunch.

Ant"

The next morning as I commenced my normal routine of lacing up my boots at 5.30am to take the coffee truck to the river, I couldn't help but smile thinking of the previous evening's events. At that point I was fully expecting a gap in communications, with a nice follow-up note from Sam to let me down gently in the next few days. In my head it would go something like this:

'Ant, I enjoyed our energetic, passionate conversation about Dear Coco and the coffee industry more broadly. However I have decided to invest in other opportunities at this time. I wish you and Dear Coco every success in your next chapter. Sam'.

I already felt like I'd achieved more than most by merely holding court with a former public company CEO for six long, productive hours. So I loaded the truck in the dark and got on with my Saturday morning, feeling proud of how I represented myself and our little business. Then on the stroke of 9.00am, WhatsApp messages starting flooding in one after the other – it was Sam. He said his mind was absolutely buzzing and wanted to confirm he'd indeed very much like to *"Step onto the ledge with me and have a crack!"* Right then I felt like the chosen one. I felt validated beyond words.

Tears rolled down my face as messages flooded in one after the other. They kept coming all day. We were throwing ideas, thoughts and insights around like we were sitting in a whiteboard session in some creative agency's boardroom. The achievement wasn't lost on me, I not only held court with a very accomplished CEO and business builder, but Sam told me Dear Coco was *the* business of all businesses he visited in London that week that had stolen the show. It was all he could think about and the volume of messages flowing throughout that Saturday reflected that. I felt like I stood in front of the investor panel on *Shark Tank* and received a record-breaking offer from the investor I really wanted to work with, and although nothing was actually confirmed yet, the moment felt incredibly significant.

Over the next seven days messages between Sam and I went back and forth, all inquisitive and exploratory in nature. It was clear he was piecing together an initial proposal and needed supporting data to refine a starting position. I had already demonstrated an open-book style of doing business to the entire coffee world, so I was very comfortable providing whatever information would be helpful – whether it be Dear Coco data or broader coffee industry intel. Days of exchanging views and ideas culminated in a second invitation to meet on Friday, exactly one week after our initial face-to-face meeting in Chiswick. We needed to discuss the initial proposal for how we might partner together. I deliberately kept this second meeting low profile with Emma, but deep down my own excitement levels were building no matter how many times I told myself its likely not going to result in anything tangible.

Friday arrived and we met digitally via FaceTime. Sam had returned to his home in Southern Europe while little old me sat at my dining table surrounded by unfinished counter signs for the following day's bakes (I'm still bitter, Coco!). The conversation started as expected – warm, familiar and full of energy. Once again I tried to elongate the amount of time we spent at the personal end of the conversation before we adjourned to business, but part of me just wanted to get straight to it. Sam got there first, saying he would be honoured to partner with me to build a Dear Coco business that's globally scalable while keeping the essence of our premium, joyful, humanised origin story intact.

Sorry, what?! YOU want to partner with ME to build a global coffee company? Holy shit, I'd done it! Please Lord don't let this be a dream.

We stepped through the high-level proposal Sam had written summarising our conversations to date, including a business valuation, company ownership structure, first-year growth targets, media and content opportunities, and longer-range growth opportunities. Wow.

Throughout the three-year, self-imposed torture of building a coffee truck business and scaling it to a global audience through digital storytelling and an open approach to doing business – I, Ant Duckworth, had just captured the attention of an investor who flew across Europe for a meeting and now wanted to partner with me 50/50 in Dear Coco's expansion. I hoped I'd never wake up from what felt like a dream, especially thinking back to the anguish I put my family through since Emma and I stood on that beach all those years earlier.

As the FaceTime call concluded we aligned on next steps which involved taking some time to do some business modelling and investment scenarios. Before the call ended I asked if I could take the mic for thirty-seconds before Sam met with the person that was currently waiting for him across the room. Here's what I said:

"At lunch last week I told you the title of my upcoming book was 'Dear Coco: The coffee truck that changed my

life'. Thanks to this little business and the conversations we've had this week, this truck has just changed my life".

I hung up the phone and cried my eyes out.

Chapter 11
Pink Lemonade and Chips

I have a recurring dream. I'm sitting around the family dinner table, I'm seventy years old and all three of our daughters are adults. Maybe there's husbands; maybe there's wives; maybe there's grandkids; maybe there's none of that. I sit quietly at the head of the table with a wry smile on my face, staring back at what Emma and I have created.

I see a family that adores each other, three women that no longer squabble over who borrowed whose blue hoodie without asking, but now look to each other as loving sisters – they treat each other like best friends. Whether they see each other regularly or not doesn't affect the love and respect they have for each other. They have their own WhatsApp group away from Mum and Dad called *Duckworth Girls*. It's filled with fun, supportive banter about all matters of daily life. Coco is part of it too, alienated for so much of her young life due to the age gap with Malia and Lani.

In this dream Emma is to my left, laughing with the girls not as an aged mum but like an older, wiser sister that still has so much in common with her girls. Emma and I have maintained a marriage so blissfully happy and strong it's the envy of anyone we meet. Our daughters see us holding hands as we walk, going on date nights, and hugging in the kitchen when no one's watching. Our relationship has withstood the test of time and is considered an anomaly in the modern world we now enjoy. This woman has been my oxygen for nearly fifty years, the person I've loved and adored so deeply we represent a bygone era of nostalgic romance.

I sit at the head of that table as someone who achieved all he set out to achieve in his life, someone who maximised his impact with the humble tools he was given. I became a man who earned his respect through hard work, determination, commitment and chasing his dreams. Through various endeavours I became a man his family looks up to, someone his girls call on for advice and the man they measure other men in their personal and professional lives against.

Regardless of my seemingly endless pursuit of money, it was never the driver of happiness for this now seventy year old, retired surfer. Money was simply the fuel that kept the family car running as we drove towards a utopia I'm now seeing right in front of me; a happy, beautiful, together family. The steely work ethic I centred my life around, the same work ethic handed down to me by my father, Paul, is now my legacy. It helped shape our girls into the kind, hardworking people they are in my dreams. Along with my stunningly happy and strong marriage to Emma, these three girls are by far my greatest achievement.

I'm asked endlessly why I put myself through what I do – why do I lace up my shoes in the dark every morning, step outside and beat myself up day after day? Why don't I just settle back with a corporate salary and find quiet happiness and contentment? Why work so damn hard as a Marketing Director, small business founder, bartender, volunteer English teacher, husband, father, friend, son or brother?

Allow me to explain. My 'why' is the feeling this seventy year old version of myself feels in this recurring dream. My version of a life well-lived is sitting at the head of that dinner table knowing I left it all on the playing field. Any athlete will tell you you're a long time retired once you pack it in, so use what you have when you have it to maximise your impact. My superpower in life is being a regular guy who does things anyone can do, but chooses not to. I've expelled energy, tried hard, never quit and loved my wife and kids like my life depended on it. I can't envisage a more maximised and admirable life than that.

~~~~~

Standing on Freshwater Beach in 2015 we didn't need to move from Sydney to London, we wanted to. We wanted a life crammed full of adventure and didn't entirely love the fact that we could envisage the next twenty years of our life playing out so vividly. Emma and I put it all on the line and away we went, without any idea how it'd play out or the challenges we'd face.

On that beach we unknowingly set a chain of events in motion that would change our lives forever. I would wrestle with my devastating, selfish decision to end the life of our unborn child against Emma's wishes. We would face significant and financially devastating immigration issues resulting in one-year-old Coco and I being stranded in Australia while Emma and the girls were homeless in London hoping I could sort it out. I'd arrive to London not able to replace the corporate salary I'd left behind and be humbled by working a more junior corporate job all week while bartending in secret to buy groceries. Hustling this hard would cause a level of damage and exhaustion my life had never known, and I'd be pushed to the brink of physical and mental collapse.

I'd wrestle with deep insecurities living a poor man's life in one of London's most affluent areas to ensure our daughters felt safe, while under-delivering on the romantic European lifestyle I promised to Emma. I'd work my corporate fingers to the bone to get promoted, before re-emptying the family's savings account to build a coffee dream that existed only in my head. We'd navigate multiple burnouts, a dangerous body image and weight loss battle with my mind, and a failed expansion into a brick-and-mortar café. I'd then be courted by a multi-millionaire investor that was so captivated by the story and brand of Dear Coco they wanted to become a 50/50 partner, invest hundreds of thousands of pounds and build a coffee empire with me at the centre.

Never could Emma and I have known the level of adventure and opportunity we would encounter, nor the number of challenges we'd face, but after its all said and done we have emerged stronger, better versions of ourselves. Emma and I set out to provide our family with a life full of adventure, and we feel immensely proud of what we've achieved together and the love and respect we continue to share.

~~~~

It's taken an incredible amount of tenacity to position the family where it is today in 2024. As a result of this hard work I now find myself in a very special position, one I've craved for five long years. Having gone without for so many years, what I crave now are life's simple pleasures enjoyed with absolute peace of mind.

Perhaps my most symbolic simple pleasure that represents how far we've come as a family is one that many people wouldn't even register as an event. On a Sunday afternoon my simple life pleasure that reflects the progress we've made is taking Lani (now fourteen) for a father-daughter date to the pub to watch a game of English football. Lani tells me these one-on-one dates with me are, and will continue to remain her fondest childhood memory as she grows older. What a beautiful thing that is. Lani doesn't want much, she just wants to spend some devoted, fun time with her dad.

These father-daughter dates fill my heart with joy, but what's even more emotional for me is comparing the current version of these outings with what they once looked like. Five years ago at the height of our financial hardship, when visiting the pub to watch football I'd ask Lani to eat before we left home and drink tap water while we watched the game. I'd buy a can of Guinness from the corner store for £1.50, stand in the pub carpark and pour it into a branded glass I put in my coat pocket weeks ago, so I didn't need to spend £6.50 at the pub. On special occasions, like when we didn't spend as much money on our weekly grocery shop as expected, I'd buy Lani a small glass of pink lemonade, but that was limited to very special occasions given how tight things were at the time.

When we arrived in London and decided to prioritise whatever money we had to live in a safe neighbourhood that we struggled to afford, our family was living off the smell of an oily rag. The financial cutbacks we had to make were immense, but also character-building. With the success of Dear Coco, the tenacity in re-building my corporate career and subsequently replenishing our life savings I can now afford to buy Lani a pink lemonade AND chips at the pub. I can also buy myself a Guinness poured by the bartender and occupy our table guilt-free.

Little does Lani know I find myself watching her enjoying these simple pleasures with a glint in my eye. This pink lemonade and chips make me feel wealthy beyond my wildest dreams. Not worrying about money to the extent I have for the past fifteen years of raising our beautiful children is a very special feeling. These kids are worth every worry, every single one – but now it's time for some respite, some simple rewards that we can touch and taste.

The Dear Coco coffee truck has shown two teenage girls what sheer will power can achieve. It's the tangible, life-changing by-product of their dad's iron will, work ethic, unbreakable spirit and relentless determination to provide for the family. If you were to ask Malia, Lani and Coco to describe their childhood from when they arrived in London I'm immensely proud to think they'd talk about the love they receive, the friends they've made, the sights they get to see and the Christmas lights along Regent Street. Emma and I have sheltered them away from the intense effort and stress that's come with our London adventure.

Our daughters are experiencing the happy, protected childhood that all parents want for their children while also getting enough exposure to understand the reality of what it's taken to deliver it. Seeing their parents work so hard to provide a life we can all enjoy has given them beautiful perspective at a relatively young age. They can sense how someone's day was by the tone in their voice when they first walk in the door, and if that tone is anything other than exuberant they'll be the first to run

169

downstairs and wrap their arms around whoever's feeling flat. Their emotional intelligence is a direct reflection of their surroundings, and they're blessed to have a family and friendship circle that shows them what kind, caring people look like.

At the time of writing, Malia is sitting her mock High School General Certificate of Secondary Education (GCSE) exams, which involves an inordinate amount of study and preparation after her already long days at school. Each night as Emma and I head off to bed we can hear Malia at her desk upstairs, diligently focused under her desk lamp writing revision cards for the next day. We're in awe of her level of self-motivation, dedication and discipline to do the best job she possibly can with the tools she has. We're all born with an inherent level of determination, and as we see Malia demonstrate such incredible work ethic and care towards her studies, I can only dream that a little bit of the way Emma and I have lived our lives has rubbed off on her.

As I get older, I think about my role as their dad. My role is ever-evolving, but what will always remain is the need for me to be their protector, provider and role model. In their impressionable young eyes I need to be undeniable in effort and conviction so when they lay their heads on the pillow at night they know their dad will never falter. That's my most important job in this life and I take it seriously.

It's said that the timeline of life is like a smile; your first and last twenty years are the upturned edges of the smile when you're at your happiest, and the sunken middle section are all the years in between. The theory goes that in the middle section (representing our thirties, forties and fifties) we have the most weight on our shoulders professionally, financially and personally. At forty-five years old this puts me right at the lowest point of the smile, so in theory I should be the most stressed, unhappy and sunken out of anyone. But you know what? I've learned to realign my happiness with the expectations of the time. Yes, I'm under immense pressure to deliver for the family financially, but I've always embraced this as something I GET to do not HAVE to do - it's a true privilege to provide for the people you adore. My most dominant emotion has always been gratitude, since I was a young boy surfing along the Northern Beaches of Sydney right through to being a coffee truck founder along the Thames in London. I own the challenges thrown at me and ensure I find gratitude and happiness within them. I'll never turn up 'tired' or 'over it', I turn up to everything I do with the energy and joy as if I'm at either end of that smile. I don't have any special powers, I'm just able to find joy wherever I can.

I'm deeply driven to leave a lasting impression on our girls, to be an example of what an honourable man might look like. The way I adore their mum, the deep respect I show towards women, how I'll protect them to my dying breath, how I remain principled in hard times, how I'm generous when generosity means we go without, and how I show strength in moments of chaos. The Dear Coco coffee truck, amongst my other achievements, merely contributes to the story I leave behind when I'm eventually gone. One of the most beautiful things to me is seeing adults talk about their aged or deceased parents with admiration and love. I can only hope the way I've lived my life can leave such a lasting impression on our daughters.

For seven year old Coco the coffee truck is more complex. As I get older my emotional walls keep coming down and I ask myself more difficult questions. *Why have I actually named this business after Coco? Do I secretly feel a sense of debt and guilt for questioning her existence before she was born? Do I over-love her as a way of saying sorry for what I did?*

As I now reflect on the Dear Coco origin story with an older, wiser heart the meaning of the business name has evolved into something much more profound. To the outside world this business is a love letter to Coco because she's too young to work shifts at the truck. But in the still of night when I'm alone with my thoughts, this business now feels like an apology letter for the shame I feel about nearly ending Coco's life in a Sydney clinic that day.

There are some things I know for certain. Demons conquered me in 2015 before Coco was born. Those demons diverted me away from the man I was raised to be by such an honourable father in Paul and nurturing mother in Maralyn. The significance is not lost on me that five years later this little girl who I had to learn to love before she was born would inspire a business that would alter the course of my life and make me the father and husband I wanted to be, but didn't know how.

On the world stage I would pen a proverbial letter in the form of a coffee truck in Coco's name – a love that that would ultimately give birth to the man I've tried to become since leaving that Sydney clinic. In the process this truck would rescue my emotional health, save our family from financial ruin, inspire a global coffee community and be named Top 5 Best Coffee Trucks in the World.

Whether Dear Coco is a letter of love or a letter of apology, both versions have propelled me forward in being the man I've desperately wanted to become; an emotionally intelligent, vulnerable, self-reflecting, protective and mentally resilient father of three. After everything I've been through over the past eight years, perhaps my most important show of strength is not telling Coco how much I love her, but admitting that I almost failed her. Perhaps the Dear Coco love letter should now read something like this:

Dear Coco, I'm so deeply sorry.
Love, Dad x

"It is not the critic who counts; not the man who points out how the strong man stumbles, or where the doer of deeds could have done them better. The credit belongs to the man who is actually in the arena, whose face is marred by dust and sweat and blood; who strives valiantly; who errs, who comes short again and again, because there is no effort without error and shortcoming; but who does actually strive to do the deeds; who knows great enthusiasms, the great devotions; who spends himself in a worthy cause; who at the best knows in the end the triumph of high achievement, and who at the worst, if he fails, at least fails while daring greatly, so that his place shall never be with those cold and timid souls who neither know victory nor defeat."

-Theodore Roosevelt

To my dad Paul.
Thank you for showing me what a stoic, hardworking man can do.

24th April 1948 - 5th March 2024
May you rest in peace.

The Code

Hopefully you'll have gathered from this book that I'm not genetically gifted, nor do I possess any special skills or talents that pre-destine me for success. I'm a regular person built exactly the same as you. My version of success has been hard-earned using analogue tools such as will power and determination. And I wholeheartedly believe we're all equally capable of achieving great things in our lives, no matter how modest our beginnings or humble our dreams.

Throughout my life I've subconsciously adhered to a set of principles that have informed how I live. I say 'subconsciously' because I've only recently become capable of articulating them. For the most part I've been invisibly guided by these principles, which have steered me to a level of success I'm grateful to have achieved. I call this set of guiding principles *'The Code'* and I'm honoured to share it with you in the event it helps steer you towards your own version of greatness. I'm confident that doing these small things day-in, day-out and without compromise will give you a competitive advantage in whatever game you're playing or battle you're fighting. I hope you find it useful.

1. Own The Dark

Your most defining, honourable, meaningful work happens in the dark away from the spotlight where no one's watching.

What each of us do in the dark sets us apart, whether it's pounding the pavement, studying for exams or opening a coffee truck. Applying ourselves to our craft out of sight from others makes us undeniable when the sun comes up. What we do under the cloak of darkness puts us at the front of the pack before our competitors have even had their morning coffee.

I decide what a winning routine looks like and stick to it without fail or deviation. I paint a picture of success in my mind and, working backwards, engineer the behaviours needed to reach my summit. I focus on small, tangible things that done without fail will be the difference between winning and losing. For example, no matter the weather or my state of mind, I'll be lacing up my shoes at the bottom of my staircase by 6.30am to ensure I'm early to the river. If I need more time to will myself into putting them on, I'll go downstairs early! There are no excuses, I simply say to myself:

"My worst day is someone else's best day, so get on with it Ant".

I'm never on time, I'm early to everything and everyone. Being intentionally or unintentionally late indicates either a lack of respect for someone else's time or your inability to manage your own. Neither of these things will make you successful or revered, so I take the opposite approach and beat everyone to the start line, always.

2. Energy Is A Choice

Showing up ready to go, with purpose and conviction means you can outperform 90% of the competition before you've lifted a finger. You've heard of a boxer winning the title fight before they've stepped into the ring – mindset and energy is everything.

We all know people who turn up to everything saying *"I'm tired!"*. I'm prepared to bet that if these same people were turning up to something they loved doing they'd show up with energy. Energy is a choice, we just need to be brave enough to choose it when doing things we don't like.

I find ways to motivate myself, understand what matters and connect the work to short and long-term goals. For example, I wanted to achieve 20,000 Instagram followers within three years of launching Dear Coco because I understood the importance of a large digital audience. I set short-term goals like posting four times a week, never deviating from my story arc or tone of voice, and taking a differentiated position in the industry. As a result, I achieved my followership goal with months to spare.

I never suffer from procrastination because I have clarity of tasks and set deadlines to deliver them. If I know I won't do something, then it comes off my to-do list immediately. If something's on my list then I'll own it, set timeframes and deliver on my promises. A former CEO boss once said to me *"Ant, people are either in or they're in the way"*.

3. Be You

You are your number one competitive advantage. You don't have to be the best; you just have to be the best at being you.

Leading with authenticity, showing openness and vulnerability has become my superpower and number one differentiator. Think about why you're reading this book, why Dear Coco has become successful, or why a multi-millionaire investor is so drawn to the business. It's all down to me being unapologetically me. There's no one like me, just like there's no one like you.

When I'm interacting with others at home or work, I'm humble, tactful and honest. Taking time to read the room and gauge the appropriate level of openness determines the degree of me they get, but they'll always get the real me. Perhaps it's my age or general level of confidence, but I have a healthy level of indifference towards most situations, which is not to be confused with cockiness. I'll do my utmost to be universally liked, but being values-driven and supported by a credible level of street smarts means I feel bulletproof – win, lose or draw. I take losses on the chin and I'm grounded enough to know that I'm not always right.

My teenage daughters say it just right, *"Dad, do you".* That's good advice.

4. Get Better

We're never done, we're never the finished article.

I'm 45 years old and will likely be working full-time for the next thirty years. I have to keep getting better, smarter and learning from the best. Whether it's in my corporate job or small business endeavours, I surround myself with the best in the business and soak up their teachings. Every day is a university day, and having a learner-mindset is a core reason Dear Coco has been successful. I'd never owned a coffee business before, so I had to figure out what world-class looked like and do things one step at a time until I got there.

The power of measurable goals shouldn't be understated.

I'm naturally a *fly-by-the-seat-of-my-pants* kind of person, but setting tangible goals has taken me to the next level. There are two key examples, the first being the Dear Coco coffee truck. Once Emma agreed to invest our life savings into my coffee dream, I said to myself I wanted to be trading by the summer. Setting an ambitious but realistic goal with tangible success gates meant I outperformed the goal and opened in May, one month earlier than expected.

The second example is this book. Typically, a first-time author spends approximately twelve months writing their first book. I set myself an aggressive target of completing the book in one quarter of that time while working two jobs and raising a family. I set myself chapter writing goals, editing goals and proof-reading goals, and I outperformed my target by two weeks. In order to achieve my goal I lived my own Code, owning the dark, making energy a choice, being me, and getting better as I wrote before, finally, being able to celebrate the wins I found along the way.

5. Celebrate Wins

Damn, this one's important. Please celebrate your wins – big or small – however you can. Humans are hardwired to perform at a high level if there's a reward available.

I'm a 45-year-old family man so my version of celebrating is no longer velvet ropes and bottle service in Ibiza! I celebrate wins with respite – luxurious time off and comforting peace of mind. I give myself breaks to put down my tools and celebrate success with family and friends.

I've never been a materialistic person, so I reward myself and my family with experiences that make us feel good. We dine out in modest restaurants, I'll send Emma and one daughter at a time to Europe for a girls long-weekend, and we give Coco exposure to fun weekend activities that make her feel special. These experiences have become my rituals for marking, remembering and maximising success. I've worked exceptionally hard over an extended period to create the level of success I now enjoy, so celebrating is crucial to success not becoming some sort of desensitised expectation.

Reading the daily habits of immensely driven people can be exhausting and make some people feel intimidated. *'The Code'* should do no such thing. Remember these are simple, actionable principles that anyone can do no matter their skillset, wealth or experience level.

I wish you immense luck and joy in chasing your own dreams. Go get 'em.

Ant

Bonus Section
How to Create a World-Class Coffee Truck Business

The allure of owning a coffee truck is undeniable. Whether it's a full-time occupation or side-hustle, owning a coffee truck is an exciting, badass way to make or enhance a living. When have you ever heard anyone upset about seeing a coffee truck on the horizon? It's like a mirage in the desert for the parched coffee lover.

However, in the interest of balance let me also say owning a coffee truck is hard, very hard, sometimes brutal. For the owner its endless problem solving and hustling, and for the barista team it's producing perfection in a cup in imperfect, challenging conditions. It's not for the uncommitted or faint-hearted, especially in a cold climate country like the UK.

According to *Barista Magazine* Dear Coco is a *Top 5 Global Coffee Truck*. This industry recognition humbles me every time I say it. We've become known to the local and global coffee community for delivering exceptional quality befitting the best brick-and-mortar coffee shops. We work with global brands on their customer engagement activations and we partner with some of the world's most prestigious events to deliver our bespoke quality at scale. On reflection it's been an unbelievable three years since launching in 2021.

While all is this important what's more valuable to me is the regard the business is held by our team, our customers and the local community. These are the people involved in our business day in day out, and without their support we're nothing more than a popsicle stand. These are the people I designed the business for, these are the hearts and minds I wanted to win, and keep wanting to delight.

After a decade in the hospitality industry followed by three years owning and operating Dear Coco, I find myself sitting on an encyclopaedic level of insight that might benefit aspiring coffee truck founders. For those with zero interest in entering the brutal world of coffee trucks, these insights might simply prove informative to hear what actually goes into putting your coffee mirage in the desert. So, in my usual spirit of sharing and transparency allow me to bring you under the hood of owning a coffee truck. Given how far we've come together through this book I've wildly abbreviated each phase of the process to hold your attention a little longer, and along the way I'll tell you how some elements translate directly into the Dear Coco business.

I hope you enjoy it.

~~~~

Phase 1: So you wanna open a coffee truck?

- **The business un-plan!** Like I mentioned right at the start of the book, I graduated university in Australia in 1998 with a Bachelor of Business. So, what I'm about to say will send my old lecturers into a tailspin!

   If no one's going to read it, don't bother writing a formal business plan!

   Let me explain. Writing things down in a fancy, professional format that you lifted off the internet won't make it happen. A blend of intuition, research, common sense and decisiveness is the secret sauce. Focus on building the business end-to-end in your mind like a storybook, obsessing over every detail. If writing things down makes you feel buttoned-up or you need it to secure investment then by all means write a formal business plan. But if it will be a twenty-page document that never sees the light of day (like most risk assessments, for example), use Post It notes dotted around your creative space and get on with it! You'll build this plane in the air no matter how you document the journey.

While planning Dear Coco I didn't write a single thing down except for revenue & Cost of Sales forecasts. This is how my brain manages projects – entirely in my head, but I acknowledge this is not everyone's style of doing business.

- **What's your model?** Crudely speaking there's three coffee truck models:

  1. Convenience – these are coffee trucks that drive around various locations. They go to where the customers are like commercial estates and high traffic locations. Picture an ice cream truck but for coffee.
  2. Deep Roots – these are street coffee trucks that occupy the same pitch day in day out. They don't move around and they embed themselves in the community.
  3. Event – these are coffee trucks built for the events industry. They primarily focus on doing private and public events at pre-determined venues. If they're not booked for an event, they don't trade.

Most coffee trucks will set aside some trading capacity for event bookings, but most businesses will largely occupy one of these categories. Depending on which business model you choose will determine the make and design of your coffee truck.

Dear Coco operates a 'Deep Roots' model. We trade exclusively opposite 85 Strand on the Green in West London and once and a while do private events (approximately four to six events a year only).

- **What's your brand identity?** If someone asks you what you stand for and you have twenty seconds to answer, what would you say? Whatever it is make it a representation of the best bits of you, and the story you want to tell through your business. The best small businesses tell a deeper story that customers can connect with. Bringing this to life through your business name, visual identity and social media presence helps tell your story at scale.

  Here's my twenty-second answer; *"Dear Coco is a love letter to our youngest daughter Coco. Given the age gap between Coco and her older sisters, who are old enough to work on the business, we named it after Coco to make her feel loved and included".*

- **Let's talk about money -** How you finance your coffee truck is a personal choice. My advice would be to set an investment limit and stick to it no matter how important an over-spend feels. Think about how long you need (or want) to pay off the initial investment before you're in-profit. In you invest an amount of money that requires more than twelve to eighteen months to pay off in full then you run the risk of over-capitalising in your business. Remember, as founder you might be working for free while this investment is being paid off, so ask yourself how long you're prepared to work for free.

I invested £40,000 of personal savings to build Dear Coco and paid it off in five months, operating three days a week, and I didn't pay myself a cent during this period.

- **The boring paperwork** – Don't lift a finger until you know what your local council will and won't permit. Understanding what you need by way of street trading licence, planning permission, health and safety certificates, risk assessments, insurance, electrical /gas certificates will inform all subsequent decisions.

I did everything the wrong way with Dear Coco, I was impatient and overly decisive. I invested all our money and started building the business BEFORE I knew all the legal requirements. I got very lucky with some margin calls that went our way but it was a risky, foolish approach.

- **Where to trade?** – For 'Deep Roots' coffee trucks like Dear Coco, pitch location will likely determine your level of success, just like the location of coffee shop. An immense amount of foot traffic is needed to capture enough passing trade to make a location viable. There will also be council and environmental conditions to adhere to, like footpath width and traffic flow. My advice is to find a pitch you like, bring an armchair, a six-pack of beer (depending on the hour) and count people walking past over the course of a week. I'd suggest that a single-barista coffee truck needs to sell 100+ cups per day on a weekday, and 150+ cups on a weekend to be viable, plus other retail sales. If you'll only capture say 5% of passers-by with a sale then you now get a sense for how much foot traffic is needed to attract enough customers.

- **Local competition** - Visit the competition regularly to assess what they do, what they don't do and where's the gap. Coffee trucks can't offer some conveniences that coffee shops do, like indoor seating, heating and bathrooms. You need to offer something they don't to make the customer trade-offs worthwhile.

- **What's the founder's role?** Think about how intertwined the founder needs to be. Without a doubt the founder should have an operational hand in the business, but whether the business can open without the founder available is a core consideration. This will inform the operations of the business such as where the truck lives overnight, who drives it to the location each day, where do suppliers deliver orders, etc. If these responsibilities sit with the founder then the business will need to close when they're away on holidays, or unavailable.

Dear Coco closes three weeks a year with our annual family holiday and my corporate travel commitments. Our home address is the business HQ so all deliveries come to the house. The business cannot run without my involvement as founder, which is a flaw and a benefit at the same time.

Phase 2: Let's Build!

- **Dude, where's my car?** – Virtually any vehicle can be converted into a coffee truck. I've seen bicycles, vintage cars, London black cabs, VW Transporters, Piaggios, Citroen HYs. FedEX delivery trucks and everything in between being converted. Understanding your business model and choosing a vehicle that suits is a personal choice. But again, be mindful of investment required to either convert or purchase your preferred vehicle versus the earning capacity of the business.

- **Inside or outside?** – Your vehicle type will inform how you serve customers. Some founders like the barista to be elevated and standing inside, others like the barista down at ground level and standing outside with the customers. The climate of your city will help inform what's appropriate to maximise customer engagement while protecting the barista from the elements.

  The Dear Coco barista stands on the street at the same level as the customer, serving out the back of the vehicle. There's also no counter between barista and customer which puts us side by side with the customer to build intimacy. We're all in it together experiencing the same thing – rain, hail or shine.

- **Workflow** – Once the vehicle type is identified be obsessive about barista workflow. Working in a confined environment is challenging enough, so make it efficient for the team so they aren't reaching over or passing behind each other. It's as simple as working left to right, or right to left with lots of pivoting on the spot.

- **Equipment** – My advice is purchase the best equipment you can possibly afford that suits the space and power source available. High-quality equipment not only produces the best product for the customer but also attracts barista talent. The best baristas want to work with the best tools. If you have to prioritise, I'd suggest focusing on the espresso machine and grinder as the main priority, while maximising other investments to the best of your ability. Your choice of equipment will dictate your credibility in the industry so it's a worthy focus.

  I prioritised installing a La Marzocco Linea Mini (at great expense due to its power requirements). But it's the best compact machine that can handle 400+ cups per day. I refused to use a LPG powered machine.

- **Want a lift?** – Understanding how far your vehicle can drive before it starts to struggle will help inform your vehicle choice. Ideally you can secure all your equipment and infrastructure within the truck and not require a support vehicle. Otherwise the morning and afternoon routine involves a support person, which for a small business isn't financially ideal, and tests relationships if you're asking endless favours!

  Dear Coco's maximum vehicle speed is 30mph so I limit the distances I travel to ten miles from home. Any further and I engage a professional transportation company to assist. Everything gets packed into large plastic tubs at the end of service and secured in the truck so no support vehicle is needed…this makes Emma very happy!

- **Let's talk about power!** – This is without a doubt the most talked about topic in coffee trucks. Crudely you have three main options: generator, mains power or solar/battery. LPG can also be used to fuel some espresso machines. The Holy Grail is mains power given its stability and consistency, but it's not available everywhere you might trade. Generators are portable and functional but come with drawbacks such a noise, odour and the propensity to stop working given how long they run each day. Solar is great in theory but often the power load required to fuel the entire coffee truck is too much without the support of batteries. Designing your overall operation to run off single-phase power (versus 3-phase power) gives you more flexibility with tapping into standard power sockets at trading locations.

  Our initial generator (£4,000 cost) only lasted eight months due to the heavy workload. I subsequently invested £6,000 and six months to get mains power installed along the street at our trading location. This was a gamechanger and we've never looked back.

- **Water** – Coffee equipment needs purified, filtered water. It not only protects the equipment from developing scale but the taste is better for the customer. Some trucks have water filters built in, other trucks filter the water as it enters an on-board water tank. The design of your vehicle will dictate the best approach, however my advice would be to ensure easy access to any on-board water filter to allow hassle-free changing.

Dear Coco uses a hose reel to pipe water into a seventy-litre on-board water tank. We purify the water through a BWT water filter before it enters the tank.

- **Choose your coffee roastery wisely** – This will likely be the business's most important relationship. If you serve specialty coffee you'll likely have access to a full-service roastery. This roastery will not only supply your beans but other products like your espresso machine, grinder, barista tools, chocolate products, alternative milks, etc. But the most important service they will offer is training and end-to-end support. If your machine breaks down mid-service, call them. If you hire a new barista and need training, call them. If you take an event booking and need more equipment, call them. If you feel overwhelmed and need a hug, call them! All other suppliers will be informed around this core relationship.

If you serve commercial grade coffee beans you likely won't have access to this kind of relationship. So you'll need to ask your friends for those overwhelmed hugs!

Phase 3: Ready to Launch!

- **What's on the menu?** Space limitations mean most coffee trucks offer a small, bespoke menu, focusing on three to four core things and doing them exceedingly well. You can't be everything to everyone, nor do you have the space for multiple grinders, endless alternative milks and arrays of food, so pick what you want to be famous for and do it above-expectation.

Dear Coco focuses on four core things: specialty coffee, bakes, little sweet shop and storytelling (which our customers get for free!) That's it, four things done to the best of our ability.

- **Training** – Training a barista to operate a one-person business is totally different to coffee shops. It's like asking a guitar player to suddenly play lead guitar, drums, vocals and tambourine all at once. There's nowhere to hide; there's no "I'm hungover today so I'm gonna hide on shots!" – the solo barista is the end-to-end experience. Training someone to deliver exceptional quality while building customer rapport in challenging conditions is not a skill every barista naturally brings. Training, ongoing support and hiring top talent are crucial.

- **Social media** – There's only so many people that can experience your coffee, so boosting your story at scale can help win new customers and event clients. Broadly there's two styles of social media feeds on Instagram; curated or raw.

  A curated feed might focus on fewer posts, high-quality imagery, thoughtful text and emotive storytelling. A raw feed might focus on behind the scenes, real-time and 'from the frontlines' imagery with short, snappy text. Here you might see the barista team throwing shakas behind the machine while the Head of Coffee plays air guitar!

  Whatever your social media style, building an emotional connection to your business with vulnerable, authentic storytelling can be powerful.

Vulnerability is not a repellent: it's a magnet that can translate into revenue if done authentically.

People travel from all over London and sometimes from abroad to visit Dear Coco because they feel emotionally connected to the business. Our social media approach also creates opportunities for me to boost our profile with podcast and media invitations.

- **Start soft** – Doing two or three soft opening days before officially opening can be powerful. With the support of your coffee roastery, quietly introducing yourself to the local community with some low-key trading days will help iron out the kinks before setting customer expectations in place.

- **What's in a name?** – Most baristas remember people by their coffee order, but asking customers their names and committing them to memory makes your customer service undeniable. Nothing makes someone feel more welcome than being greeted by name, so doing this exceeds expectations and creates sticky customer relationships.

  For the first five-months of Dear Coco I wrote down every customer's name with a description of the person in my iPhone notes (for example, *Brad – nice Aussie bloke, big muscles*). When Brad re-appeared in the queue I'd sneak a look at the list and greet him by name, it was so powerful.

- **Build the team...at the right time** – When the time comes to hiring a team, setting the culture from the top is everything. When hiring ask yourself if this person will lift the culture (if so, hire them), maintain the culture (if so, develop them) or erode the culture (if so, walk away from them). They need to care about this business almost as much as the founder, so choose wisely and be generous with your recognition and reward.

Phase 4: You're Open!

- **No Dickhead Policy!** – Lots of coffee trucks don't have a physical front door, they're out in plain view. As a result some people think we're "on their turf". Priority #1 is protecting the barista team by having a firm *No Dickhead Policy*. We can't kick customers out and close the door so they need to visit the truck with respect or not visit at all. Tolerate no one.

- **Good morning!** Be uber focused on winning the morning coffee routine of the local community. This is the most protected and lucrative coffee service of the day, and it's the hardest one to win given it involves a gamble from the customer to break their established routine. Once you have it, keep it through exceptional product and service.

- **The 'Credibility Stock Exchange'** – Consistency in coffee trucks is vitally important. If customers aren't sure whether you'll be open they won't take the risk, they'll head straight to their brick-and-mortar cafe. On those unruly days where the weather is horrible and you'll make no money - turn up and show commitment anyway. This trades your stock on the Credibility Stock Exchange and you'll win over the long-term.

- **Event bookings** – These are a great way to expand your reach and diversify your revenue streams. Finding the right number of events to take without causing too much disruption to your normal trade is key. For non-event trucks I'd suggest no more than 10-15% of your trading capacity assigned to events is about right, but it's your call.

  Dear Coco limits ourselves to four to six marquee events per year, strategically chosen to maximise revenue and brand impact while limiting disruption to our street coffee customers. Customers are generally happy to see you off making extra money through event bookings, but don't push the friendship too far!

- **Over-pay your baristas** – Coffee trucks are hard places to work, especially in cold climate countries. Baristas should be rewarded for the challenging conditions and operating your business singlehandedly. The minimum wage in the UK at time of writing is £10.42 per hour, and Dear Coco pays our baristas £14.50 per hour to acknowledge these additional challenges of working at a coffee truck.

- **Be my guest** – Running a lean team is important to manage costs, and having a small brigade of guest baristas who work in other coffee shops is helpful. They are fully trained in your business and can fill roster gaps if the founder can't work the open shifts themselves. Barista temp agencies like *Baristas on Tap* or *Need A Barista* aren't ideal given the nature of a single-barista operation and no colleagues to work alongside to learn the ropes.

- **Become a Meteorologist** - Learning the impact of the rain and wind, and how to minimise its impact is vital to protecting your team and equipment. Angle the truck into the elements to protect the barista, close doors to shelter the team while still being operational and ensure out-of-sight goods are upsold by the barista. Whatever you need to concede to protect the barista, do it and well-trained barista will help minimise the financial damage of battening down the hatches.

- **Give a shit!** - Be part of your community, support local initiatives and embed yourself in the community. Don't let the fact that your venue has wheels and rolls away at the end of each day sever the roots you put down. Locals will support you if you add something to community while still extracting money from it.

Phase 5: The Daily Grind

- **The 1%ers** – A coffee truck founder largely operates in the shadows, doing invisible effort away from the spotlight. Being self-motivated to do the small, unglamorous jobs every day is what separates the good from the great. Be undeniable, do the work and you'll be rewarded with relative riches and enormous street cred.

- **Be active on socials** – Post regularly and religiously, be open and vulnerable about the realities of business and life - sugar coating is for the uncourageous. If your storytelling needs you to stray away from coffee and talk from the heart about a broader issue, just be you.

Dear Coco curates four to five posts a week on Instagram, plus daily stories to keep the algorithm working in our favour and our followers engaged. I'm also a contributing author for FLTR Magazine to deliver long-form content to a broader coffee industry audience. Vulnerable storytelling and creating emotional connections is how I roll, hopefully you've felt this throughout this book.

- **Cheer each other on** – Fellow coffee truck founders wind up becoming colleagues within a lonely category. You will be alone, but don't feel lonely. Use social media to cheer each other on, visit other founders if you can and show your support – you'll make their day. More broadly be part of the coffee industry and be curious. Without day-to-day colleagues to learn from its important you find other sources of knowledge.

- **Maintain a winning culture** – No matter the challenges faced, and there will be many – make your culture immovable. Whether its team or customer culture, never move the line when faced with adversity. Be generous in times of hardship, supportive in times of chaos and calm in times of panic. How you behave in moments of crisis is how you'll be remembered.

- **Budget for the unexpected** – Mark my words, you WILL face unexpected challenges that mean you're going take a financial haircut. Concede defeat and budget for two to four zero revenue weeks per year. This will take the panic out of the situation when it happens.

Dear Coco budgets for being open forty nine weeks a year.

- **Know your numbers** – There's money to be made in coffee trucks. Margins are very different to a coffee shop, and if done properly can result in a healthy net profit for the owner. But with the financial upside comes with risk of significant loss given how exposed coffee trucks are to elements outside our control, such as weather and equipment damage/failure.

Allow me to bring you behind the curtain into our business and share Dear Coco's Chiswick Truck financial performance for 2022. For comparison, net profit for many brick-and-mortar cafes might range from 5-15%, in 2022 Dear Coco achieved 40%.

Dear Coco Chiswick Truck, 2022 Financial Performance Trading period: 49 weeks, 5 days a week Amounts in GBP		
	GBP	**% of Total Revenue**
Total Sales	**£144,560**	
Pitch Fees (Rent)	£1,100	<1%
Business Rates	£0	0%
Wages	£27,500	19%
Utilities	£1,560	1%
Coffee Costs	£18,792	13%
Bakes Costs	£10,119	7%
Milk Costs	£4,336	3%
Disposables	£4,550	3%
Miscellaneous Costs	£1,331	1%
Value Added Tax (VAT)	£17,347	12%
Net Profit (GBP)	**£57,925**	**40%**

My parting words: BE OBSESSIVE! Obsess over the details and have a blast…it's coffee and cake, we're not saving lives.

Happy brewing!
Ant x

About the Author

Ant Duckworth is a father, husband, Founder and CEO of Dear Coco Coffee, renowned storyteller and former Marketing Director for global brands. He is contributing author for FLTR Magazine, a world-leading specialty coffee publication.

Ant lives in London with his wife Emma and three daughters Malia, Lani and Coco.

Author's Credentials

- FLTR Magazine: 1st and 3rd most popular feature articles of 2023
- FLTR Magazine: 2nd most popular feature article of 2022
- Instagram @dearcocolondon: reached 50K+ followership as one location and growing fast. Connecting to a global community with a vulnerable, transparent, open-book approach to storytelling.
- YouTube @dearcococoffee: home to Inspire & Educate, Dear Coco's place to tell richer stories. A living breathing video album of Dear Coco moments as Ant & Sam build the world's next great coffee company and hero entrepreneurship.
- LinkedIn: www.linkedin.com/in/antduckworth/ 4K+ followership. Connecting to a global business community with an open book, share-all approach the small business entrepreneurship. Most popular post (themed 'Credibility Stock Exchange') exceeded 4.5M views and 47K engagements.

Industry Credentials

- Named Top 5 Global Coffee Truck, Barista Magazine 2022
- Most attended main stage session at London Coffee Festival 2023
- Featured in Pretty City London (print and social), Barista Magazine, Perfect Daily Grind Magazine, FLTR Magazine (4 feature articles), Sprudge Magazine, La Marzocco Global Interview Series, London Coffee Festival, 2nd Renaissance Podcast, Storians Podcast, Have You Eaten Yet? podcast, @manmakecoffee (leading global coffee industry community).